IT'S NO LIFE FOR THE WIFE

Judy Almond

Best wishes

Judy

IT'S NO LIFE FOR THE WIFE

Printed 2001
Reprinted 2005

Published by Judy Almond
1 The Forge, Coopers Lane,
Northaw, Potters Bar,
Herts. EN6 4NF
e-mail: david.almond7@btopenworld.com

ISBN 0–9549463–0–8

Printed by IntypeLibra London Ltd
Wimbledon SW19 4HE
e-mail sales@intypelibra.com

Jacket designed by Jon Paine Graphic Design
2 Varcourt Place N.W
Calgary, Alberta T3A 0G8
e-mail jonpaine1@home.com

This book is dedicated to

Dr. Rodica Matusa of

Constanta Hospital, Romania, and

all the children in her care.

ACKNOWLEDGEMENTS

My sincere thanks are due to my long suffering family and friends, and especially to my dear husband David, without him there would have been no book. To Anneka Rice who brought the plight of the Romanian children to our attention, and to Bill Hamilton who did the same for the Albanian children. To my nephew for designing the jacket, and Sam Suresh and Jane Rogers at Intype for their help and patience.

Acknowledgements and thanks are also due to:

David Grubb of "Feed the Children" for allowing me to print his two poems THE HOME and THE ROOM.
Bill Hamilton ALBANIA WHO CARES? published by Autumn House 1993
Ralph Barker GOODNIGHT SORRY FOR SINKING YOU published by Collins 1984.

A special thank you to Sue Morgan Jones for use of some of her many photos of the Romanian children, to her husband, Major Graham Jones MBE for the successful visit of the Lancers' Band, and to them both for their continued involvement, support, and friendship.

And finally to those of you who buy this book or send a donation - every penny will go towards equipment or medicine for the clinic in Constanta - so the biggest thanks of all.

For more copies, please contact the author at:-

1, The Forge
Coopers Lane
Northaw
Potters Bar
Herts
EN6 4NF

Books cost £7.99 plus £1.25 pp.
Please make out cheques to Judy Almond

2nd book now available:

"I'm Here To Help Now, Dear."

This second book is written to raise money for
the surviving children, now teenagers, to give
them a chance at a future. Price etc. as above.
Thank you for caring.

Chapter 1

Patience and Patients
* * * * * * * * *

They say your life flashes before you, but all I could think when I found myself the wrong end of a Kalashnikov, held by an Albanian with death on his mind - mine - was "He can't kill me, I'm a grandmother." But it was not until I was dragging David out of a sewer in Patagonia on our 37th wedding anniversary that I began to think my famous friend was right.

"It's all your fault, darling" she said, as she poured her tea into a saucer for her peke. "You attract trouble. I feel sorry for poor David, in fact I feel sorry for most husbands these days." This coming from the Queen of Romance, Dame Barbara Cartland, with over six million books sold on the course of true love was certainly food for thought.

I would be the first to admit life with David has not been dull. As secretary to one of the Queen's physicians and his partner when I met David in 1958, I already had a glimpse of what life must be like married to a doctor in general practice. Even David's proposal should have alerted me. Although I was ill with glandular fever he still hauled me out of bed and marched me up to the top of a local beauty spot to propose. Very romantic, but it was all rather lost on me as I was feeling so poorly, so I asked him to give me some time to think. "Don't be long," said David, "I've just accepted a job with a practice that wants a married doctor."

After a whirlwind engagement of six weeks, during which time I saw David at the most half a dozen times, we were married, with my mother still worrying about whether he was "all right".   This feeling of unease arose from his socks which never matched, they were not just different tones of grey or blue, but patterned with plain, and maroon with navy.   The overall appearance was not helped by the socks having repeatedly been sent to the hospital laundry, which pinned a piece of tape on them each time, so one could not help one's attention being drawn down to his feet, what with the different colours, a fringe of tapes, and numerous glittering safety pins.   He was finishing a midwifery job at a London hospital and for six months he had been on duty for 36 hours on and 12 off (if he was lucky) and at the end of it I don't know whether he knew night from day, much less sock from sock.

Anyway, there I was married, in a strange part of the country some considerable way from friends and family and with no transport.   In 1958, before the advent of the various clever answering services, a GP was virtually forced to marry to get a job.   I am surprised the marriage service for doctors' wives did not include the promise to love, honour, obey and answer the telephone for ever and ever.   David threw himself into his work with his usual enthusiasm.   As the newly joined assistant on trial to the practice he got everything the rest did not want, and having specialised in midwifery he did most of the deliveries, many of which in those days took place at home.

People were very kind though, and whether it was out of a sense of duty to ask the new doctor and his wife round to dinner, or because they genuinely wanted to make us feel welcome, invitations started to arrive. I soon found out which were which. A brief look at me with some polite small talk over pre dinner drinks, then David would be pinned down mercilessly over dinner for a consultation on various ailments troubling host and hostess. I did not mind too much as the dinners were usually good, and David was still new and fresh enough at his job not to mind working morning, noon and night.

One evening was especially like this. Our host and hostess, a Mr and Mrs Cummings, oozed charm over David when we arrived, but I was almost totally ignored, and when we sat down to dinner the medical inquisition started. In fact our host had almost undressed by the end of the second course in his eagerness to show David various parts of his anatomy. I had managed to get in one or two acid remarks about how nice it was to come out and forget medicine for a bit, which were beginning to sink in at least where Mrs Cummings was concerned, and it was quite apparent we were not destined to be friends, when the telephone rang.

It was the local midwife for David to say that one of his mums was well on the way. "Shan't be long" said David, "It's Mrs Trent's fourth, she'll pop it out like shelling peas in no time, save me some cheese and I will be back for coffee".

After the bustle of his departure silence fell over the table. Stilted conversation followed while mine host struggled back into his shirt and jacket and we tried to make the cheese spin out. After about an hour it was decided we would have coffee at the table. Mr Cummings poured himself a stiff brandy and soda, and Mrs Cummings declined the offer of a liqueur on behalf of us both. I felt this was a mistake as it might have sweetened the atmosphere between us, but I suppose she must have seen me punishing the wine during dinner through sheer boredom .

We floundered on till midnight struck, and then it was suggested we move into the back room as the heating had gone off.   At least the chairs were more comfortable, in fact Mr Cummings fell asleep almost as soon as he sat down, and for the next hour his snores rose up.   He had already explained he could not drive me home as his car was in for servicing, and no way was I going to walk three miles through dark streets to the other side of the town.   Mrs Trent was not on the telephone to find out what on earth was happening, so we sat, Mrs Cummings and I, and sat and sat.

Finally at one thirty there was a knock at the door and there stood David, beaming away.   "Slight hitch," he said, "but all's well that ends well, and mother and babe are fine".   Thankfully I got into the car, and David leaned across to give me a quick kiss and say sorry.   I was just about to say I quite understood when I caught a distinct whiff of toothpaste, and then noticed a bit of a pyjama top peeping out of his shirt. "Ah," said David, "Well, I can explain that - things took a bit longer than I thought.   I drove back past the Cummings place which appeared to be in darkness, so I thought you must have gone home.   When I got back home I found I hadn't got a key, and knowing how cross you are if you have to get up and let me in, I got out the ladder, climbed up to the spare bedroom window and got in that way.   I undressed in the bathroom, cleaned my teeth, and it wasn't till I climbed into bed I found you were not there".

"Never mind," he went on.   "I expect you enjoyed yourself."

One of the things I missed most during our first year of marriage was the occasional bunch of flowers of our courting days. I had a bit of a moan about this on our first wedding anniversary, and the following week David came home with a lovely bunch of expensive flowers. I was delighted, but felt guilty about the cost. A couple of weeks later he arrived home with an even more expensive looking sheaf of flowers, and I was quite overcome. Two more flower arrangements followed at intervals of a few weeks, and by this time I was really worried about the expense, but David assured me I was worth it.

All became clear when I had to ring the local hospital to leave an urgent message for David, and Matron said how pleased she was I did not mind having some of the funeral flowers they got left with, as so many people were too superstitious to have them in the house. David says this is the first time he realised there is no pleasing women.

There were other perks to be had in those days. David had managed to cure our local cinema manager of some complaint no one else had had much success with, and in return we had free seats any time we wanted. We could transfer the calls to the box office if anyone was due for delivery and the usherette would come and find him if he was needed. Hissed messages would be passed along the row, "Nurse says Mrs Smith is three fingers," definitely a sign of imminent delivery and off David would go. As he climbed back along the row some time later he would be put through a third degree on the sex, weight and condition of the baby, and the information would be relayed round the cinema. All a bit different now. I grumbled about the broken nights, the parties I never got to, or got left on my own at, and the drain a difficult confinement was on David, but perversely, when babies started to be delivered in hospital I missed not being the first to know that Mrs Knowles had had a girl after four boys, and that after all the fuss Mrs Jones made during her pregnancy she had sailed through her labour. I missed being stopped in the street and shown babies by proud mothers who said it was all thanks to my husband, although I must admit such statements overheard by strangers could have been misconstrued.

In spite of all the extra work and hours David really loved this part of his work. To deliver a healthy baby safely, and be part of the delight and joy of the family, acted as a counter balance for all the illness, suffering and death he was usually involved in. At long last the Medical Schools are now including training on dealing with terminal illness and death. To mention death has been the last taboo. When a doctor is obliged to deliver a death sentence it requires great sensitivity to gauge to what extent patient and family really want to know what is in store. Recently the establishment of Wellwomen and now Wellmen Clinics, and the increase in preventative medicine has helped to provide an alternative to dealing with just illness and death, but for many years after babies had to be born in hospital David missed the contrast. A few years before he retired babies began to be born at home again, and he had the pleasure of delivering babies for mothers he had delivered, although few and far between are the doctors prepared to risk the responsibility of home confinements in these days of high insurance and litigation.

Another message that could have been misconstrued was on a card attached to a lovely ornamental tree which arrived outside the door one day.

It was from a lady who wrote "To Doctor, in grateful thanks on the death of my husband." Luckily I knew it was because David had allowed her husband to die in his own bed at home instead of shipping him off to hospital, even though it meant visiting him sometimes twice a day, and towards the end, during the night as well.

Other things arrived on the doorstep, specimens of urine in various bottles, which used to get a bit mixed up towards Christmas in particular when grateful patients left bottles of whisky for doctor. This was due to various television sagas about doctors at that time where they only ever seemed to drink whisky. In those impoverished years we could not afford the ginger ale to go with it so I had to hold my nose to drink it neat until I did a deal with our local off licence to swop the odd bottle for gin and some tonics. I had to be careful though; one year I tried to swop a bottle of whisky not noticing that on the front was a message "In grateful thanks" from the local undertakers.

I found the transition from a busy working life commuting to London and going out to the theatre or for a meal in the evenings, to being tied to the telephone most of the day, rather hard. I tentatively suggested I might look for a part time job, but this was greeted with absolute horror by David's partners. There were five in all, the senior partner worked on his own, two shared a surgery in the High Street, and David and another partner worked from the lower end of the town. Surgery hours were from 8 a.m. till 11 a.m., when the doors were shut. Visiting was done till evening surgery at 5.30 p.m., then the doors shut at 7.30 p.m. There were no appointments, and if there were 20 people or more still in the waiting room when the doors shut the doctors stayed till they were all seen, quite often this could be 9.00 at night. There were surgeries on Saturdays, and when David first joined, the senior partner had only just been persuaded to give up a Sunday morning surgery. Eventually he allowed the other partners to share the nights on call, so David only did one night a week and every other weekend. During the week the telephone would be through to the surgery during surgery hours, but once the doors shut the wives had to take over, and for the nights and weekends their husbands were on. No payment was made for this slave labour until a few years later it was discovered that doctors were allowed to claim payment for mistresses to answer their telephones, but not wives; mistresses, unlike wives, could not always be expected to be in the Doctor's home or bed, apparently the proper place for a wife according to the tax man.

Later on with many more female doctors their other halves could not possibly be expected to answer the telephone, having careers of their own, and so the answering service was invented. Do you detect a faint trace of sarcasm? You would be right. When I suggested sharing the telephone between the five wives during the week, leaving only one day a week to stay in, and sharing the five weekends between the five doctors, leaving only one in five on duty, you would have thought I had suggested the overthrow of Queen and country. Even one of the wives thought I had gone a bit far. At the annual Christmas get together that year her only remark to me was that the sooner I got pregnant the better. It was then I took a closer look at the other wives. One had six children, two had four and one had three. Was there something in David's contract which said all partners and their wives had to produce a certain number of children? When tackled he seemed a bit vague about it, but said it would be a jolly useful thing to do, to have a baby, then I could give first hand advice on how to cope with pregnancy and new babies to the patients when they rang up.

With the coming of spring I realised I was pregnant, and having had nothing whatsoever to do with babies or small children I found it all rather scary. As a doctor's wife I found that I was supposed to know all about babies and how they were born, and did not like to confess my ignorance. The partners all thought David was looking after me, and David, if he gave it a passing thought at all, imagined one of the partners would take care of me. Eventually someone realised I had better go and sign on with the local obstetrician, who unfortunately felt that first babies should be born in hospital, especially first babies of doctors' wives. "They always seem to have complications," he said cheerfully.

I was not happy about having my baby in hospital. Having sat for an hour waiting to be seen I had noticed all the glass cases filled with unmentionable looking instruments, and even worse ones in his consulting room. I felt if I could have it at home I would be safe from these instruments of torture. "At home? Under no circumstances." David's immediate partner's face was quite white when I put my request to him. Still, I had the last laugh. David caught mumps from one of his little patients and I caught the mumps from David. Still infectious when I went into labour I could not be admitted to hospital in case I infected everyone else!

Although grateful to have the baby at home I cannot say it was a very pleasant experience. It would have been better if David could have stayed with me, but in those days it was not done for the husband to be there, and anyway he had to take the surgery while his partner was with me. Whether it was the mumps or not I found I had no milk at all, and the baby had to be put on the bottle. This did not go down well with the senior partner as he said it was much easier to take messages while breast feeding a baby as one had a hand free to take them down.

When I had my second baby, another boy, two years later, I was determined it would all be different. For a start there was no opposition to having it at home, and I was given a list of things to have ready, and a large cardboard box only to be opened by the midwife. The list was a bit off putting, and included a nail brush, a jam jar, scissors, needle and thread, and a pile of newspaper. A friend who was heavily into dogs said it was just the sort of things she had handy when her bitches whelped so not to worry. I also armed myself with my own personal birthing equipment. A do-it-yourself book from the National Childbirth Trust, a large whisky and well-practised breathing exercises. In fact they were so well practised and worked so well I had difficulty convincing David around 2.00 a.m. that the baby was coming.

Eventually he rang for the midwife only to find she was already out on a call, but he assured me the pupil midwife would come. She had no car and came by ancient bike, so by the time she arrived she and David were still at the polite "Can I take your coat?" stage, when I was well into the second stage of labour. In fact when I could attract any attention David went into instant overdrive, diving under the bed and wrenching out the box, furiously throwing a snow storm of sanitary towels out and shouting "Hold on, hold on, you are supposed to be sitting on a sterile sheet!" This time the senior partner was miffed as the baby was born without the presence of any of the other partners.

Third time round, two years later, and it was David who was determined to get it right, so when I started into labour in the night he sent for his partner, the midwife, and two pupils. They all arrived very promptly and just as promptly at the sight of all the expectant faces round me the contractions died away. We sat and looked at each other till dawn when I got up and cooked breakfast for them all and they went their separate ways. David went to Saturday morning surgery, his partner retired to the spare bedroom for a sleep, and the midwives went off on calls. They all re-assembled for lunch, and after I had cleared up I left them sitting in front of the television to watch the Cup Final while I retired for a well earned rest. Without a ring of expectant faces round me I did very well, and I left it a bit late to attract any attention from downstairs, especially as there had been no score and they were into extra time. I don't need any other proof of David's love when I remember how he dragged himself away just as West Ham scored the winning goal, and he delivered our third son as the final whistle went. Slightly drunk with elation I insisted on cutting the cord myself as I felt I had done most of the work unaided, and I made a short speech along the lines of "I name this baby etc." This time the senior partner was only miffed because West Ham had won.

All of this of course made me an absolute authority on pregnancy, child birth and child rearing. What it did do was make me far more sympathetic to panic stricken mums who could not cope. I can distinctly remember the shock I got when I changed my first born's nappy the day the cord dropped off, saw a spot of blood in his navel, and rang most of the emergency services, only stopping short of the fire brigade. Those awful towelling nappies, lined with muslin, from which the lumps had to be scraped, the whole wad of nappies covered with unyielding rubber pants. And the regulation winceyette nighties with tapes to tie down the back, always in a knot. One's day was ruled by the washing, especially without a washing machine. My first washing machine was a 1934 Beatty, bought for £5 when my second son was born. Visiting Canada a few years ago, I went to a museum in Calgary where to my amazement I saw among the exhibits a 1935 model. Mine was a magnificent machine, a gleaming steel tub on lion claw feet, with a paddle that could have powered the Queen Mary, and an electric wringer balanced on top of the tub. It took all the hot water in the tank to fill it, and had to be emptied by a hose attached underneath and run outside the back door. By the time the last load had been fed in, paddled, and wringered into the sink, the water had acquired a well used look, especially if something had run, and the neighbours used to look forward to the flood of rainbow coloured water that whooshed down the side entry into the road. My next door neighbour in particular, a married woman of some 50 years, felt bound to keep an eye on me and give me the benefit of her experience.

She used to worry if my washing was not out by nine o'clock in the morning, apparently only sluts and hussies were late hanging out their washing, and if doctor's underwear appeared on the line a pale green, blue or pink, or whatever the colour of the day was, she got very upset. She also advised me to watch doctor's kidneys, she had "seen them exposed" when he was bending over, digging in the garden. She was always hinting at some dire and unmentionable disease she suffered from, and finally plucked up courage to pass me a very screwed up piece of paper from her glasses case on which was written "Visceroptosis". That, she told me in a hushed whisper, was what she had suffered from all these years. I had not the heart to tell her that all it meant was slack stomach muscles.

The telephone continued to be the bane of my life. Some days it seemed to ring non-stop, and it was very difficult to take a proper message from an incoherent mum holding a screaming baby when my three were all yelling for their long delayed lunch. Before the days of the mobile phones I then had to ring round the list of David's calls to pass the message on. Whether the patients liked it or not I had to ask for details of their problem so David could decide which was urgent and which could wait till he fitted them in. There were always the awkward ones who, when asked what the matter was, said if they knew they would not be ringing the doctor, which was not a lot of help to me! A man rang up in a great state one day and said Grandpa was dead. I asked him his Grandpa's name and address, but he was in such a state he said he could not remember and would go and ask his wife. Minutes later he came back to the phone and said it was all right, the old boy had only dropped off for forty winks.

Although I was always ready to give advice over the phone if I could, as someone totally untrained medically I always ended up by telling the person to ring back if they were still worried, or if my advice had not worked. Quite often all it needed was someone to talk to and who would listen sympathetically. One of my small triumphs was when a mother rang up and after much hesitation burst out that Penelope's pee was pink. Knowing that Penelope was four I asked whether she had been eating beetroot, and she had. It just so happened I had read an article in the "British Medical Journal" about beetroot colouring young children's pee pink. I felt obliged to keep up with the latest articles in the BMJ, just as I felt obliged to watch Dr Kildare and various other medical sagas on television. Whatever the illness of the episode people would ring up the following day suffering from the same symptoms. It also behove one to read up on any advances in medicines or medical equipment in the Readers Digest, as someone would be sure to ring up and ask to swallow the latest mini-camera, or have the latest in magic valve replacements.

Mind you, weaning some of the older patients off their bottles of coloured water and on to the newer pills for their complaint David found quite difficult. In our town, 14 miles from Hyde Park Corner, he had patients when he first came who only had gas lighting, and had never been out of the town. Not all his new ideas were greeted with enthusiasm among relatives. One old boy had been a semi-invalid most of his life having been told he had a weak heart as a child. David put him on some new pills and told him to get up and enjoy life. Which he did, enjoying every minute, living for a further 10 years, and spending most of his life's savings.

In the middle of a 'flu epidemic I had been answering the phone for about 36 hours non-stop. When it went again in the middle of the morning I picked it up in a daze to hear heavy breathing, and a voice then said he would like to rain hot kisses over my entire body. "Oh yes," I said, "Name and address please," which he meekly gave. I have always regretted the fact I was too tired to go round!

We used to have a hostel in the town for men whom my grandmother would have referred to as a halfpenny short of a shilling, which I think is much nicer than what is probably politically correct now. One night David was called round to see old Joe, who was a heart case. When he got there, he was greeted by one of the others and told "Not to worry Doctor, the lads are working on him." They certainly were, there he lay on the floor with one man pumping his legs up and down, and another giving him the kiss of life by blowing in and out of his ear.

I got things wrong as well, especially when it came to all the various coy names people use for normal bodily functions or parts of their anatomy. One message I had to pass on was certainly short and to the point. "Tell doctor my parts as parts are useless." Another lady sounding desperate shouted over the screams of her child that her little boy had caught his little tiddly in the door and she dare not look to see what the damage was. I got David from another call to go round right away. When he got there, sure enough little Jimmy was all doubled up and screaming fit to bust. "You will have to take his trousers off so I can have a proper look" said David. "Why take his trousers off to look at his little finger?" asked the puzzled mother. Another distraught mother rang to say her boy was stuck on the lavatory. I thought she was talking about him having constipation, but it turned out the plastic lavatory seat had split under him and caught a bit of his buttock. Every time he tried to stand up it gripped him tight!

Chapter 2

David's Biggest Mistake
* * * * * * * * * *

It was after the birth of our third son that David made what was to be his biggest mistake. Years before, during my last term at school, there was an opportunity to go to pottery classes. I only joined at first because it meant a walk into the town on a Monday afternoon to the local Art College, but I found I really loved it. Most of my vases on the wheel turned into rather crooked egg cups, but I did model a horse which I was very proud of as it was chosen for the Festival of Britain Schools exhibition on the South Bank. Fired by this I wanted to do something with art when I left school, but my mother wisely sent me to St James's Secretarial College in London as she said this would be of more use to me later on.

I went to a few evening classes before I was married, but afterwards, tied to the telephone and then the children, this was no longer possible. So when David saw an advertisement for a second-hand potters wheel he bought it for me. This was to be the end to a fairly peaceful and organised home life. A wheel is no good without a kiln to fire the pottery in, shelves are needed to stack the green ware before it's fired, and then more room to store it when dipped into the coloured glazes to wait for a further firing. More space is then needed to show the finished ware in order to sell it, as once in full production it is far too expensive to keep giving away to friends.

To my delight and David's surprise people wanted to buy my pottery, especially the local flower arrangers, or the Begonia Mafia as David would call them. There was a vogue for Japanese flower arranging at that time, luckily for me. Put simply it meant using only a few flowers and twigs, but placing them at special angles which all apparently meant something, like Earth, Heaven and Man. The pots, made up of various unusual shapes with holes at the right angles to put flowers and twigs, were a challenge and a pleasure to make.

Telephones, door handles and saucepans rapidly acquired a coating of clay. As the children grew out of waking in the night, sitting up to watch the kiln reach the correct temperature before it could be turned off, took the place of getting up to them. David had to buy a shed for all the equipment, and he quite often volunteered to 'kiln sit' if he was on nights, especially in the winter when the shed got lovely and hot, but I could not guarantee he would not fall asleep propped up on the side of the kiln, or get called out at the crucial moment. The second firing, the glaze one, was always the most exciting as terrible things could, and did, happen. If the kiln got too hot the glaze would flow down and stick the pots to the shelves, if not hot enough the colours would not develop. It took two or three days to cool down sufficiently to open the door and peep in. Open it too early, especially if it was cold outside, and fearful pinging noises could be heard as the glazes crazed.

I enjoyed making the pots, and it was nice to earn some money, even if it only covered the outlay on raw materials. It also meant I was not so resentful at having to be tied to the house. About this time I was involved in helping with school visits to stately homes, and I was disappointed at the lack of nice things to buy in their shops, mostly only personalised tea towels, dusters, key rings and ash trays. I felt it was a shame there was nothing better to sell, especially when you consider that the shops were usually situated in the kitchens and still-rooms of these great houses. Women in days gone by would have produced all kinds of interesting and delightful things; reading about their lives in such places I was amazed at the resourcefulness of these women. They were responsible for the health and well-being of the family with no GP to call out in the middle of the night. On their skill in preserving, drying and storing food for the winter would depend the lives of the weaker members of the family. Only a hundred or so years ago women could make soap, polish, candles, paper, cloth, perfumes, ink, cheese, butter, preserves, bread, ales and cordials to name but a few of the items. They would grow and prepare the herbs and flowers needed for all the various recipes, for pot-pourri to freshen the rooms, sweeten the linen, keep away insects, and promote sweet sleep, for the pomanders and nosegays to ward off infection and for the various teas, infusions and medicines.

I felt that this sort of knowledge, acquired over the centuries by trial and error, was worth taking note of, and decided to try my hand at producing some updated items from the old days starting with herbal teas.

I had great fun reading through the old herbals, eventually concentrating on the ones by John Gerard written in 1597, and that of Nicholas Culpeper, 1652. I reluctantly left out anything described by Pliny the Elder from the 1st Century BC, or by Dioscorides from the 1st Century AD. As it was, some of the suggestions by Culpeper and Gerard as to what the teas would cure needed some censoring, especially those referring to sexual or gynaecological problems. My final selection of seven teas were chosen mainly to take into account ease of obtaining the raw materials and their cost, and to cover a broad spectrum of "cures". I knew I had to be very careful with the wording on the labels (David went quite pale at my first attempts, and went even paler when I tried the first brews on him). Luckily I had no idea of the minefield waiting for me if I wished to market and sell products of any sort, much less those for consumption, and this was well before the EU and Common Market. "Fools rush in where angels fear to tread" was written with me in mind.

I rang up the local Trading Standards Department, and, explaining my problem to six different people all of whom thought I was quite batty, eventually found dear Mr Cheshire. He was to become a friend and confidant over the next few years, sharing many a cup of coffee (no, NOT any of that herbal muck PLEASE) in my kitchen, and who was to help me stay out of the clutches of his own department. David was proving a bit jumpy about the General Medical Council, so I did not want to put my name and address on the labels, only permissible if the goods were pre-packed at home and distributed from there, which they would be, so that took care of that. I had read somewhere that the cost of packaging some products far outweighed the cost of the products themselves which I thought was a bit steep, so I had decided to use plastic bags with cardboard headers, each header a different colour and with the appropriate information on it for each tea.

Filling the bags was not too bad, but getting each

bag with exactly the same quantity in it using a tablespoon was impossible, and weighing each one was out of the question. After all, I had my sights set on the mass market. However, Mr Cheshire assured me that "In relation to the marking of weight, this can be avoided if the teas are pre-packed in a quantity of less than 1/2 oz. Any quantity above 1/2 oz. must be marked with its weight and made up ONLY in one of the following quantities: 1 oz., 2 oz., 4 oz., 8 oz., 12 oz., 1lb or a multiple of a pound." Surprisingly, none of my teas were intended to be more than 1/2 oz., and if they just happened to be so I reasoned I could not be jailed for giving extra weight.

Under the need-to-know principle I did not inform David of all of this, and Mr Cheshire and I worked out a perfectly satisfactory form of wording absolving me of claiming any miracle cure for the teas along the following lines: "Sage is said to be a tonic, Mint to aid digestion, Camomile to soothe the nerves, Elderflower to expel colds, aches and pains, Thyme to relieve coughs and asthma, Lemon and Savory is cheering and anti-septic, and Orange and Basil is said to cleanse the palate and comfort the heart. True or not they make a delicately scented drink which is both refreshing and healthful. Today people are rediscovering the simple natural flavours of herbal teas." When I think this was in the late 1960s, I feel I had a hand in starting the herbal tea trend!

I had also come across references in the history books to Elizabeth I's addiction to hot spiced red wine, liberally laced with sugar, which was said to have rotted her teeth and not improved her temper. David entered into the tasting sessions with much more enthusiasm than he had done with the teas, and I finally came up with the definitive version of Mulled Wine Mix, the recipe known only to me and Elizabeth I, a blend of spices and sugar. This was followed by a Mulled Ale Mix, much favoured by Pepys who was always plunging hot pokers into foaming tankards. This last idea was greeted with scorn and disbelief by some of my friends; I was delighted when a few years later, browsing through an Antiques Fair, I came across a copper object which the man assured me was a Mulling Slipper for ale. This was in use in most pubs until the demise of the open fire after the second world war. Beer was poured into the "slipper", ginger and sugar added, and the long pointed toe part was pushed into the fire.

In packaging the two mixes in clear plastic bags like the teas, with pink for wine and brown for the ale cardboard headers, there was only one snag. Unlike the teas, which kept in their contents when the header card was stapled on, the mulled mixtures, being mostly sugar, leaked out. This was before the days of the re-sealable bags, but heat sealing was just coming into being. An engineering friend was persuaded to put his mind to my problem, and came up with a soldering iron mounted on a hinged stand. The bottom of the soldering iron had a bar welded on to it which heated up enough to seal the top of the plastic bags, although the timing was crucial. Too long and the plastic melted, too little and the stuff poured out. I trained David to its use, and he proved extremely deft at getting it just right. I also allowed him to be in charge of mixing up the spices and sugar, and spooning the stuff into the bags. He said he felt his nine years of medical training had not been wasted, but as I pointed out at least he could sit and watch Match of the Day while he did it, although at particularly exciting moments some packets got a bit extra spooned in.

The first Elizabethan era was one of great expansion, particularly in the City, and merchants traded throughout the known world. They founded Guilds of Craftsmen, jealously guarding their various trades, and building fine Halls, many of which stand today. One was for the Candlemakers and Tallow Chandlers. Until the introduction of paraffin wax in the l9th century the poor had made do with rushes or rags dipped in tallow, or even rotting oily fish like herring or mackerel to provide light. Only the rich could afford the pure beeswax candles, and with the founding of the Candlemakers Guild rules and regulations were laid down as to who was licensed to make them and how. In Tudor times they were not dipped, but sheets of beeswax were warmed and rolled round a cotton wick, the thickness of the sheets to match the number of strands of cotton in the wick to form an even-burning candle.

It just so happened that I had recently acquired a hive of bees. Knowing that I was a soft touch when it came to anything small, furry and homeless I had been talked into giving a home to a hive of bees, surplus to someone's requirements. I was assured they would be no trouble; all I had to do was sit back and wait for the honey. I passed this information on to David who was not convinced, and told me to get a book out on bee-keeping as he was sure it was not that simple. My youngest son took my words to heart and spent a considerable amount of time sitting by the hive with a spoon, waiting for the jars of honey to roll out of the front. David was right of course, the book was full of various things one had to do, including putting in fresh sheets of wax, already marked out like honey comb, for the bees to pull out and fill with honey.

The bee-keeping did not turn out to be a success, but I found a source of sheet wax, and tracking down cotton wick followed the instructions to "warm ye wax till it cracketh not, and roll round ye cotton", or words to that effect. Warming the sheets of wax on top of the boiler I produced the first prototypes. I bet you did not know that to produce one pound of wax bees have to make six to seven pounds of honey, which means roughly 37,000 loads of nectar to each pound of honey produced, and the mileage flown to gather enough nectar is approximately 50,000 miles or twice round the world. Which is why wax candles have always been so expensive, and why, whenever possible, the wax combs are put back into the hives to save the bees having to waste precious honey producing the wax. I tried to explain to my son how the bees produced the honey, that pollen and nectar mixed with enzymes in the bee's stomach were regurgitated into the comb as honey. He immediately lost interest in waiting for the jars to appear, as he said he had no idea that honey was just "bees' sick". To produce wax, bees take in great draughts of honey, and then hang themselves up in a living sheet. Slowly droplets of wax ooze from the pores in their abdomen which they scrape off and use to build the combs. This information also did not go down well.

David was not a success as a beekeeper, although I gave him perfectly clear instructions from my book from the safety of a nearby bush. I admit the first swarm he had to take could only be reached from the top of a tall ladder, but he could at least have hung on to the skep when he knocked the swarm into it, instead of dropping it on my head. Opening the hive to extract the honey was also a very fraught time, and David got badly stung, so badly that he had to give himself an injection and stand in the shower for half an hour. We all breathed a sigh of relief when a local beekeeper took them off our hands, but at least as I said to David it gave me an in-depth understanding of beeswax candles.

So there I was, armed with three quite professional looking lines, the herbal teas, the mulled wine and ale mixes, and the beeswax candles. The next thing was to find a market.

Working on the assumption that it is better to start at the top rather than the bottom I took my courage in both hands and wrote to various owners of stately homes. Shortly afterwards embossed and crested envelopes started to fall heavily through the letter box. Leaving the letters around to impress was not a success, as my middle son wanted to know why railway stations were writing to me, various Dukes, Lords and others being in the habit of only signing their last name, Salisbury, Wellington, Bedford etc. Summoned to Woburn with my first small order I splurged what small profit there was on having my hair done, and a new outfit, just in case I saw Himself. Not only did I see the Duke, but he was charm itself, congratulating me on my products and told me that opening one's home to the public was not all glamour, it was mostly providing teas and toilets! The Duchess was not available at that moment, having a bit of bother with a large consignment of black bead necklaces which she had bought while on a trip to Africa, and which had been stored in a damp outhouse to await the opening of the house and shop. With some warm Spring weather the beads had started to hatch out small black beetles, and there was a crisis meeting going on with inspectors from the Environmental Health Department and Ministry of Agriculture. I left the Duke muttering darkly about the way to hell being paved with good intentions.

Other orders swiftly followed, and Hatfield House insisted on having some of my pottery as well if I could produce something small and easy for visitors to carry, especially overseas ones. I started to turn out some little posy pots, but was already finding that although my spirit was willing, my body was not. It just could not cope with heaving lumps of wet clay around, on top of large boxes of shopping, and wearing a neck brace did nothing for the confidence of David's patients when I answered the door. In any case, I had hardly sent off repeat orders of the mixes and candles before they were wanting more, and through the network of stately home owners yet more "railway stations" were asking for price lists and then ordering.

By the time that first season ended I realised what a market there was, and worked flat out through the winter in every spare minute making up stock for the start of the next season. In those days most of the houses only opened from Easter to the middle of September, so I thought I would have enough of a breathing space to catch up. There was a snag though; money was not something it seemed quite right to mention, and payment could anyway not be expected till a month after delivery, however early one had to pay for the raw materials.

The Latin mottoes of some of the stately home owners when translated by David made me laugh, "Late but in Earnest", "What I have I Hold" - I decided mine would have to be "Cash on Delivery", but it proved almost impossible to enforce. In an effort to bridge the cash-flow gap I started to have a stall at local craft markets. In those days they were few and far between, and the standard of the products was high. No bought-in goods were allowed, and the items for sale definitely had to be of one's own design and/or production. It not only helped considerably with the cash flow, but enabled me to try out new lines on the unsuspecting public.

It was the beginning of the pot-pourri era, and I had great fun devising my own mixtures using quite a lot of material from my own garden. David got used to picking his way carefully through sheets of newspaper covered with leaves and petals in various stages of decay, but the boys moaned a bit at scented gravy. I found the essential oils extremely strong, and so they should have been at the price. When you consider it takes 50,000 rose buds to produce an ounce of essential oil I suppose it is not surprising. Drying scented material, however strong to start with, evaporates the essential oils, so they have to be re-introduced without causing the dried material to go mouldy. To do this you have to use a fixative such as orris powder, the ground up dried root of the perfume iris, or for a cheaper version dried ground orange peel will do. The commercial pot-pourries mostly use synthetic oils and fixatives, which, while giving an instant punch, do not in my mind compare with the delicately and carefully made scented bowls of pure ingredients found in the stately homes. Just running the hands through a properly made pot-pourri will release the perfume, even if it is many years old.

It soon became apparent I needed a bigger quantity of dried material than I could get from the garden, but luckily I found that the importers I got my herbs from for the teas could also supply me with what I needed. I settled on four varieties, Rose, Lavender, Lemon Verbena, and a mixture, Elizabethan, which was rich and spicy. Having used up all the scraps of material in the house to make smelly sachets, I had to track down a source of cloth, lace and ribbon. I found everything I wanted in that emporium of the East, Brick Lane, an Aladdin's cave of treasures. The snag was that one had to buy wholesale, which meant rolls of cloth, cards of lace and drums of ribbon. And I needed a different co-ordinating colour for each of the four "flavours". Splurging the previous season's profit and some of the housekeeping, (Brick Lane does not believe in anything other than cash) I bought four rolls of beautiful flower sprigged cotton with matching ribbons and lace.

Yet another snag, with the best will in the world I could not manage more than two rolls at a time home in the tube. Poor David. What he regarded as a little hobby to keep me nice and quiet, was turning into a full time job for me and quite an involvement for him. However, he was quite nice about giving up his half day to collect the stuff, but wished I had found somewhere easier to collect from than Brick Lane.

Carried away by the sight of all the lovely material when he brought it back I started to design and make up more and more scented items, hangers, night-dress cases, hanky and tights cases, even scented hotwater bottle covers. In a way it was forced upon me, there being an average of 30 to 50 metres in a roll of material, and the sachets only taking 9 cms by 9 cms it would have taken a long time to shift 200 metres.

Packaging presented no problem; I made the products fit the standard size of polythene bags in each case. This saved me a lot of expense as I could buy the bags off the shelf, although as time passed and I began to use them in the hundreds rather than dozens I had to find the source, an obliging firm in the Isle of Wight. I had little cards printed to go in each item telling people how to refresh their pot-pourri when it faded, preferably with my little bottles of essential oils which by then was another line, and to the horror of my boys headed the cards "Another Scentsation from Judy Almond". I thought it was quite neat, and all the scented items sold like hot cakes.

My only real trouble was that I had bullied some of my friends into doing the machining, as I was a complete failure at anything that needed sewing. It had taken me two weeks of frustration to produce the first few samples. Much as they enjoyed the money it fetched, as the orders mounted they became more and more overwhelmed with work. I looked hopefully at David, but decided I was pushing him quite hard enough in other directions, even knowing his skill with the needle at the minor operations he performed. Using one's friends in this way is the quickest way to lose them, so I advertised for home workers. After one or two false starts, (one lady machined beautifully and quickly, but the scented items came back each time smelling of the fish she cooked each day for her five cats) I found four who formed the backbone of my "cottage industry", sharing in all the ups and downs of the next few years.

One out-worker called Jean asked if she could roll some beeswax candles as well as doing some machining. I was glad of the help as orders for those were multiplying, but had to think of an alternative method of producing them. The basic method was just as they had been produced in Tudor times, the sheet of wax warmed till it was malleable, then rolled round a cotton wick and left to harden again. I had been using the top of the boiler to start with, but this meant the boiler had to be kept going full blast. Someone had to have a bath, or a load of washing had to be put in to keep it working, and the boys and David proved a bit reluctant to take baths at strange times of the day.   I then pressed into service the electric plate warmer that we had been given as a wedding present, and which had never been used. This proved nearly ideal, but got very hot so you had to be jolly quick at rolling otherwise you were left with a sticky mess of melted wax. It worked better with a tea cloth laid on top, and it was then I had the brilliant idea of trying David's photographic dryer. He had a spasm of developing his own photographs in the early days of our marriage, before the boys were born, and had rigged up the downstairs lavatory as a dark room. He said it was just right, as he could hang the developed photos for rinsing in the loo, then they went onto the dryer, a metal hotplate with a thick cotton cover attached. Just right for rolling candles and luckily David had gone off his photographic hobby, especially now the loo was being used for its proper purpose.

Jean did not blink when I added another candle, short fat, to the standard range, and she doubled her turnover. It was some time before I discovered it was her husband who had taken over making the candles. He was a long distance lorry driver, and liked nothing better than "soothing his nerves" by sitting and watching telly and rolling candles. I was to be very glad he had joined the team when a well-known High Street chain contacted me, and after a meeting with three obviously very important people in my boardroom, i.e. the kitchen, an order was placed for 3,000 short fat candles.   I was most impressed with these people.   I had to explain that with handmade items a large order did not mean they would be cheaper. It was not a question of programming a machine to produce more, in fact it would probably mean a bonus of beer for the lorry driver, and sherry for my various friends who would have to be pressed into service. Also there was the nasty gap between buying the raw materials, having them made up, delivering them and getting payment.   My reluctance to accept the order seemed to make them even keener, and it was agreed that I could deliver 1,000 at a time and would be paid promptly for each delivery so I could buy the next load of wax and wick.   How I wish all my customers could have been so reasonable and understanding, and I also wish there had been a happy ending.

Unfortunately they did not tell me that they were going to have the candles bubble- packed two at a time in a beautifully designed box using the latest commercial technology.   The machine to do the job was only able to function on exactly the right measurement, with no allowance for any minute alteration in size.   They had taken just one sample with them and used it to set up the clever machine.   As each candle was individually hand rolled they all came up a little differently, which luckily I had pointed out at the meeting, and they had said it was part of the attraction. Even more luckily they had the decency to admit they had said it, and insisted on paying me for the 3,000. This did make me wary of taking on large orders without examining the problems which might arise very carefully, but still did not stop me getting into two further situations later on which could have ended my career as an entrepreneur. One was when the National Trust ordered 500 items but put an extra 0 on the end. 5,000 of that particular item I knew from experience was going it a bit even for the NT to sell, but they got quite cross when I kept querying the amount, and even crosser when they got 5,000. After a bit of a battle we eventually reached a settlement, and I took quite a few items back, but it left a bit of a bad feeling. The other situation was even worse when I accepted a nice large order for an assortment of items in the run up to Christmas, and as it was so close to December 25th sent the whole order instead of asking for payment for half the goods at a time, especially as they were a new and unknown customer. I did check their bank references which were fine, but as the fraud squad said when they called on me, they were professionals. Over tea and tears in my kitchen the inspector warned me that bank references are really not worth the paper they are written on, and made me feel better by telling me of some of the big companies these particular villains had conned. Apparently they slap in a big order just as the rush is on, sell the stuff off cheap, mostly in street markets and off the back of lorries, and do a runner before they are caught up with for payment. They then set up the scam again in another area and with other firms the next Christmas.

Something else which did not turn out quite right was the first (and last) appearance of my candles on TV. The owner of a large and beautiful stately home in Kent was not only a gifted musician but a collector and restorer of early pianos and harpsichords. His recitals on various instruments given in the great hall of his house were very popular, and he was invited to appear on television to give a recital on one of his early Victorian pianos. As it had brass candlesticks he decided to use my beeswax candles to give it an even more authentic appearance. I wish he had asked me first. One of the features of rolled beeswax candles is that they do not drip, but this is only if they are burnt out of a draft and upright. All went well to start with, but gradually as the recital progressed, the heat from the television lights began to soften the beeswax, and to his horror they not only started to bend over the key board but to drip. Worse was to follow. As the wax hit the keys, it started to solidify and stick them together. The last piece he played was luckily by a fairly obscure composer, and he said afterwards he just hoped no-one noticed the lack of a few notes in the top and bottom registers.

I felt the time had come to put the business on a more professional footing, especially as I had some of my products chosen to be included in the Design Centre catalogue. I was really proud of this, but it did not seem to make much of an impression on David and the family, nor my immediate friends, who just wanted to know if I was still making my "little things". I had to enlist the help of an accountant, who entered into the spirit of it once he had got over the shock of my book-keeping, and the fact that I kept all bills out in one carrier bag, and all payments in, in another. I could never understand how he managed to make what I considered a perfectly straight-forward system into such an incomprehensible jumble of book-keeping jargon, but apparently he and the tax man understood it. He did tell me that as I had to pay tax at the top whack, because my earnings for some reason were added onto David's, I should take advantage of the various allowances. For one thing I was entitled to put expenses incurred while up in London or elsewhere collecting materials or meeting prospective customers against my profits, and I could also claim 'protective clothing'. Once we had ironed out that this did not mean a sandwich and a cup of coffee, or in the case of the clothing a new expensive winter coat, I joined the ranks of the expense account lunching fraternity, and only had to stop when I got too fat.

This was before the dawn of the jet-set woman business executive, and to start with I found it rather intimidating to have lunch on my own in some smart restaurant. It was then I found that marvellous institution, the Foyle's Luncheons. They were held at the Dorchester in those days to celebrate the launching of a famous author's latest book. The chairman would give a witty speech introducing the author and he or she would then give a short resumé of the book and how it came to be written. Not only was it always extremely interesting, but the surroundings were elegant and the lunch extremely good. The paying public sat round tables holding twelve, and depending on the attraction of the main speaker and book there could be from 5 to 35 tables. The long top table was reserved for invited guests and friends of the author or Miss Foyle, and always included various celebrities from show business, the arts or Parliament, many of whom would also give a short speech. Some of the speeches were not quite what one would have expected. I remember Patrick Moore giving us a resumé of his new political party and nothing about his latest book. The Duchess of York did tell us all about Budgy the Helicopter, but also announced she was pregnant. This did not stop David Frost, who was chairman that day, from smoking an enormous fat cigar all over her at the end of the meal. Recently, instead of Norma Major telling us about her book on Chequers, her husband held the floor and had us all in stitches with tales of behind the scenes at Number 10. And it was difficult to sort fact from fiction when Edwina Currie came to talk about her latest bodice ripper.

To actually see and hear these famous people was fascinating, and just as fascinating were the people I found myself sitting next to during the lunches. One elderly lady, in a black sequined toque had been coming to the lunches since before the war. We started off on the wrong foot as we were both seated that day on the last table. Turning to me as I took my seat next to her she said, "This table is usually reserved for late-comers or nobodies. I am a late-comer, which are you?" I had to admit I was a nobody. A sniff was the answer and obviously that was going to be the end of the conversation for the rest of lunch, but at that moment one of the stately home owners passed on his way to the top table and, spotting me, took the opportunity to save on a stamp or phone call and asked me to get in touch. My standing immediately went up several notches with my neighbour, and in the course of lunch she told me about her travels when first married. Her husband took her on various long-distance flights. Going to Australia took nearly three weeks travelling in a large flying boat. There were armchairs and a dining room on board, and landing on various lakes and oceans they then stayed in hotels overnight. They also travelled right across Africa in a much smaller aircraft, and made several forced landings among herds of elephants, rampaging lions and hostile natives.

Members of the press attended these lunches,

and on one occasion I found myself sitting next to someone from the Guardian. I had been a bit pushed for time before leaving home that day. For some reason I was trying to dye a piece of material a special blue, and in my haste was stirring it round with my hand while I read the instructions. Too late I noticed it said, "Always use a stick or metal spoon to stir the colour into the water." I tried to keep my hand out of sight, but he noticed and wanted to know why it was bright blue. One thing led to another and I told him a bit about my cottage industry. He seemed most intrigued and before I knew it had booked to come and interview me. Even being entertained in the power house of my industry, the kitchen as usual, did not put him off, and I was written up on the business page of the Guardian. Even my mother believed in my "little things" then, although David had to put up with some of his patients saying that perhaps if he could not cure them his wife's herbal teas might!

It was about this time that my famous friend came on the scene.

Chapter 3

My Famous Friend
* * * * * * * * *

Not everybody has a famous friend, especially one like mine, so I am afraid I am inclined to boast a bit. The beginnings were not auspicious. I was in the middle of getting supper for the three boys when the telephone rang.

"Somebody answer that," I shouted from the kitchen. Back came a shout from the hall "It is some woman who says she is Barbara Cartland." As far as I was concerned it could either have been one of David's patients who had finally flipped her lid, or a friend having me on, but when I got to the phone I heard a voice I was to get to know well say "This is Barbara Cartland here. I understand from my hairdresser who lives near you that you make little things." As I was now supplying most of the stately homes and cathedral shops in the country, the National Trust, and exporting to 14 countries I suppose that about summed it up.

"I am always looking for good quality gifts, something a bit unusual but reasonably priced," she continued. Quickly checking how long it would take me to tidy up and set out some "things" I asked her when would she like to pop along and have a look.

"I do not," said the voice emphatically, "pop anywhere." However, she went on, she would send the chauffeur to collect me and my "little things" and I could come to tea the following day.

In vain I explained there was a medical

conference in progress and as we had a Canadian doctor and his wife staying, it was my job to entertain her while the conference was on.

"Quite all right," was the reply, "You can bring her as well." And down went the phone.

Next day at 3.45 p.m. precisely a white Rolls Royce arrived and the uniformed chauffeur loaded an assortment of boxes and bags containing my little things into the boot. My Canadian visitor Dorothy had been in a state of nerves ever since being told where she was going for tea, and had spent the last hour changing into different outfits for my inspection. At this point I think she would have gone back and changed into her evening dress if I had not firmly pushed her into the back of the Rolls where she sat murmuring "Oh my God, they are never going to believe this" quietly to herself.

We drove down the lanes and through the turquoise coloured gates into Camfield Place. The house itself is very imposing but is not that old, having been rebuilt in the 1800s on the site of a much older house. Beatrix Potter lived there at one time, and there is a walled garden which surely was the domain of Mr McGregor. And plenty of rabbits digging up the lawns everywhere. As Dame Barbara was to tell me later, she dared not have anything done to control them as somebody was sure to say they were the descendants of Peter Rabbit. She had already been threatened that acid would be thrown at her if she continued to wear her fur coat - "Just think, darling, what they would do to me if I had Peter Rabbit's great grandchildren done away with?"

An efficient secretary welcomed us, helped the chauffeur in with the boxes, and we were shown into a large spacious drawing room, with floor-length windows overlooking lawns sloping down to a lake. The room seemed filled with flowers, on pedestals in the windows, and on gold-legged marble tables set on a pale turquoise carpet. The long sofa and chairs were in a deeper turquoise silk, and everywhere there were exquisite pieces of china of the shepherd and shepherdess style. In all it was the perfect setting for one of Dame Barbara Cartland's romantic novels.

At that moment in she swept, firing a volley of orders to yet another secretary scurrying along behind her. Then in her early 80s, she moved with the speed of a woman half her age. Swift introductions, during which Dorothy, I swear, started to curtsey, and then we were borne off to the dining room for tea, collecting on the way a Pekinese who showed an unnerving interest in my ankles.

The dining room, all in deep red and lined with ancestral portraits, was filled with a vast long table, and right at the end was laid tea for three. A beautiful silver tea service, fine bone china cups and plates, cucumber sandwiches the size of postage stamps, a gooey-looking chocolate cake, various home-made biscuits, and two large meringues reminded me of the sort of tea we used to have when I was small. I also remember the slap on the hand I got from my grandmother when, as a child, I picked up a similarly sized sandwich at a polite tea party, and put it straight into my mouth. "You must always put it on your plate and then make it last two bites." So when offered the cucumber sandwiches I struggled desperately, with teeth well past their best, to bite through the one slippery piece of cucumber in the little sandwich. I then noticed our hostess popping them straight into her mouth!

Meanwhile a butler appeared to hand round the

tea, and another man came in and started crawling round the edge of the room. "He's from the telephones," said our hostess airily. I tried to keep up with her flow of conversation and make intelligent responses, both on my behalf and Dorothy's as she seemed struck dumb, when suddenly Dame Barbara said "You are both doctors' wives aren't you?" Round my cucumber sandwich I nodded. "And you look in your forties, so you must have finished having children?" Another nod. "Well, have you had your wombs out yet?" A feeble shake of the head from us both. "You must tell your husbands to recommend it to all their patients. Have your wombs out, start on hormone replacement therapy" (which in those days was the first time I had even heard of HRT) "and take the vitamins I shall recommend and you will be new women. And," she added "your sex life will improve no end."

At this point I noticed the man from BT had come to a halt, although the butler, who appeared to have heard it all before, continued to hand round the plates. Luckily Dame Barbara did not wait for a reply, and hoping Dorothy's mouth would close of its own accord, I foolishly accepted one of the meringues I was being pressed to have. "The chef made them specially, he will be very upset if you don't have one." How often was I to hear that. I have never had the nerve to tell her I hate meringues, especially the poor chef's, as they are large and hard and shatter all over the table and down your front immediately you try and bite into them. At one time I thought I had cracked it by feeding the Peke bits under the table, but one day I gave him rather too much, and she noticed white crumbs all round his mouth.

Apart from enquiring after our wombs, she gave

us a very firm lecture on the dangers of over-prescribing of tranquillisers by doctors, especially to women who were suffering menopausal symptoms, and a very concise and pithy report on the pay, conditions, and standing of midwives, all of which she felt needed improving.

On the dot of 5.30 yet another secretary appeared with an overflowing folder of letters to be signed. "Come along," and Dame Barbara was up and away into the hall while Dorothy and I were still struggling out of the soft embrace of the sofa. "I shall look at your little things when I have time and be in touch sometime next week if I find anything suitable," she said, and pressed what turned out to be two autographed Cartland romances into our hands, beautifully gift-wrapped in bright pink.

At this point I tried to get a word in edgeways that I needed the samples back the next day, but with great charm and the remorselessness of a Sherman tank we were eased out into the Rolls.

The return journey was mostly silent, except for the occasional "Oh my God" from Dorothy, or it could have been from me!

This was the start of a friendship with Dame Barbara over the past 18 years or so that has been fascinating, exhilarating and on occasions nerve-wracking, but never boring. Always in great demand for interviews by television and radio from all over the world, she keeps four secretaries fully occupied with the hundreds of letters she receives and answers personally each week, and in taking down the 5,000 words she dictates each day of her latest novel.

She is a celebrity among celebrities, and her business interests are world-wide and varied. She is

President of the National Association for Health and promotes alternative medicine. In 1988 she was invited by the Prime Minister Rajiv Gandhi to fly to India to open the largest health resort in the world near Delhi. I remember the occasion well, as she rang me up a few days later to ask me to come down for a chat as she was in bed. "Are you ill?" I enquired anxiously. "Well," she said, "The doctor says I have something called jet lag, so I have to stay in bed for a couple of days." At the age of 87 she had flown out to India on the Friday, spent two days promoting the resort, giving interviews, talking about alternative medicine, and being feted by the Indian Government and officials, then flown back home on the Sunday night.

Her designs, called "Decorating with Love", for the National Home Furnishing Association are sold all over the U.S.A. She has written over 600 books and is in the Guinness Book of Records for that and the fact that she is the best selling author in the world, having sold 650 million books. Her books are translated into 23 languages and so far four books have been made into films and videos. In 1991 she was made a Dame of the Order of the British Empire, not only for her contribution to literature but for her work for charitable and humanitarian causes.

In spite of all this she has never lost sight of what life is like for the rest of us. Calling in on her late one Christmas Eve she could see I was in a bit of a state. It was my turn to have David's large family for Boxing Day, and I had just collected the turkey. Not only was it the only one left, but it was much smaller than I had realised, and the piece of ham I had cooked that morning had shrunk to nothing. The shops were shutting and I just could not think what I was going to do.

"Don't be feeble, darling" she said, and summoning her chef told him to get two brace of pheasant out of the freezer for me. "Defrost those overnight, pop them in the oven with the turkey, and don't forget to do lots of baked potatoes to fill them up." I know you could say it is easy to be thoughtful when you have a chef and a freezer full of pheasant, but I doubt it would occur to many people to help out like that.

One of her recurring problems which I do enjoy helping her with is making up numbers for her lunch or dinner parties. She is quite superstitious about sitting down 13 at the table, and as she likes to have 12 or 14 if possible, it is not surprising that she is sometimes left at the last minute with 13. This is where I come in. With David quite often working at the weekends she knows I am usually available, even at short notice. I must say I always enjoy myself even if it is a bit nerve-wracking.

On one particular Saturday David had a morning surgery which meant a late lunch, but at least I could sit and have a quick read of the paper before I went shopping. I decided that in the interest of the endless battle against the bulge I would cycle the four miles to the market. My bike has panniers on the back that take a surprising amount; just as well as I do tend to get carried away with market bargains. A friend drove past me after one of my more successful expeditions and thought from the back I was a decorated float, but who could turn down bunches of gladioli at that price?

Unfortunately on this particular day a steady drizzle started on the return journey and by the time I reached home I was extremely wet. Adding to the chaos I had left in the kitchen I had started unloading the panniers when the phone rang. Still dripping I snatched it up to hear a familiar voice - "Darling, where HAVE you been - I have been ringing you all morning, it's TOO bad of you - you are never there when I want you."

"Now look here, darling," she continued, "I need you to help me out. I have one of my rather special house parties here this weekend, and I am having a few extra people coming in to dinner tonight, but I am left with an odd number, so I want you to come as well to tidy up the seating plan. Tell David I am sorry there is no room for him, but I am sure he will not mind" she added firmly. Of course I said I would be delighted.

"Lovely darling, now be here at 8.0 sharp, and I have Royalty so don't forget to bob, they still expect it. And it's full fig, so wear something long and pretty, and I hope you have not had one of your awful short hair cuts, it makes you look dreadful and years older than you need. Bless you darling, see you this evening, you are an ANGEL to help me out." And down went the phone.

As I stood there I happened to catch sight of my hair in the mirror. No, I had not (thank God) had a short hair-cut, but the wet wisps hanging round my face made me wish I had. I also began to take in what she had said. For a start the hairdresser was shut for the weekend, and a quick mental check of my wardrobe did not unearth a single item or collection of items that could be termed long, or full fig.

After a nerve-calming cup of coffee I plucked up my courage and, phoning her back, started to explain about my hair.

"Now darling, don't be so silly. Come at seven

o'clock and my hairdresser can do something with it."
And down went the phone again. By this time it was
well past two and I had to get David something special
for lunch while I thought about how I was going to
break it to him he would have to take his calls on his
bleep and not via me, something he hates. I consider
the bleep the best advance in medicine since the
Hippocratic oath was thought of.

Having convinced him he would quite enjoy an
evening on his own, struggling with 15,000 patients, all
of whom have the potential to make his life a misery, I
finally got upstairs about four to start the search for
something suitable to wear. Emptying the wardrobe,
loft, and sack of clothes waiting to go down to the
charity shop I narrowed the field down to a turquoise
silk cocktail dress. Two things were against it, it had a
straight high neckline in front although it went into a
deep V at the back, and it was only knee length. My
famous friend likes women to look feminine, and hates
high necklines along with short hair. "You have a good
bosom, darling, show it!" I have been told.

Getting frantic I found that if I turned the dress
back to front I could achieve the desired effect, which
only left me with the length. If I wore my short waist
length black silk petticoat around my thighs instead of
my waist it reached to my ankles, and standing in front
of the mirror it looked quite effective under the cocktail
dress. I found to my cost later that it rode up when I
tried to walk unless I developed a short shuffle, and as
for a low curtsey - forget it. However, Dame Barbara
had said a "bob", so it was hopefully only minor
Royalty.

A hasty bath, into the outfit, on with every
available bit of sparkling jewellery and I was ready.

David said he thought I looked super when I showed myself to him for a final inspection, but as he did not raise his eyes from the newspaper he was reading it was not much help. It was also not much help to realise he would be unable to drive me to the party as he was on duty, so I would have to drive myself in my red Citroen van.

When I got to Camfield Place the Rolls and the Daimlers had taken up the best parking spaces, but not wishing to slosh through any more puddles I managed to squeeze the van into a space right outside the front door. The maid helped me to pull down my petticoat and I was shown into Dame Barbara's bedroom to be "seen to" by her hairdresser. At least the first steely glance from Dame Barbara at my person did not draw any adverse comments, and after my hair had been got at even I was impressed. However, when Dame Barbara was unveiled from various layers of nylon capes she stood revealed in a skin tight strapless sheath of diamante, topped by the biggest diamond necklace I have ever seen. The maid added similar sized earrings and a bracelet on each wrist, and the hairdresser added the large rings on her fingers. It reminded me a bit of the knights being dressed for jousting in medieval times, but if ever I get to ninety I hope I can look as glamorous. And as thoughtful as ever she insisted I had a glass of champagne before we went down stairs as she said she knew what a rush I would have had to get ready.

Down the stairs we swept, with me bringing up the rear like one of those tugs behind the QE2. I was worried about how I was going to get across the hall and into the drawing room without resorting to the shuffle I needed to adopt to keep the petticoat in place, but I was pleased to see that, because of the skin tight diamante sheath Dame Barbara was reduced to a similar shuffle. Several couples were already assembled in the drawing room, and she gave us all a quick briefing on the house guests, including the Royal Person, and a couple of Princesses from various obscure Balkan States, - "And don't forget to bob." One woman was so overcome I noticed she even bobbed at the butler when he came in with the drinks.

The Royal Personage turned out to be a charming man, and luckily, when I found myself next to him, I remembered to ask after his daughter, who had been mown down on the ski slopes and suffered a broken leg. And it was not me who put their foot in it by saying "Bloody German wasn't it?" as some rather pushy chap did who wanted to join our conversation. As the House of Windsor is probably more German than British it went down like a ton of bricks.

The only sticky moment for me before dinner was when Dame Barbara's son, who lives on the estate, arrived to join us and demanded to know in a loud voice why the postman had abandoned his van right outside the front door. Dinner went by in a blur of trying to talk, eat, and cope with the half-dozen glasses being filled in rapid succession in front of me. Dame Barbara does not like people to hold the table up by eating slowly; she seems able to talk nineteen to the dozen and eat with speed herself, so it behoves those of us who sit down the far end of the table and get served last to start eating when the meat or fish hits the plate without waiting for the vegetables. One's plate is cleared, empty or not, when she gives the signal.

This can catch out those not in the know, as it did a man who sat next to me at a shooting lunch and who, aghast at my table manners, waited very pointedly till he was served not only his vegetables but the gravy as well before picking up his knife and fork, only to have his plate removed before he had time to eat more than a mouthful. To give him his due he then said I must have known something he didn't. Unfortunately, at this particular luncheon this good impression was spoilt when the cheese was served and the decanter of port came round. I love port, and as the only two glasses left unused by that time were a large glass for water and a tiny glass for a liqueur, I greedily poured myself a large glass of the ruby red liquid, only to discover it was in fact cherry brandy. My neighbour was most impressed. He said he liked women who could handle their cherry brandy like that, but I was having trouble getting my breath back and wiping the tears from my eyes. My grandmother would have said it served me right.

For dinner parties it is always the custom, as in Edwardian times, for the ladies to leave the men to the port, and to retire to freshen up. For me this is another sticky moment, as it is my job when given the nod from Dame Barbara at the other end of the table to get the ladies my end to leave the room to the men, their port, and their stories. Not something the modern young woman is used to. Then I shepherd them upstairs to the second-best bedroom and loo while Dame Barbara whisks more important ladies, anything these days from a Prime Minister to an Ambassador, to her room. We re-assemble in the drawing room for a good female gossip before the men re-join us, but not before Dame Barbara has hastily told us to move apart and leave room for the men to sit among us. "Otherwise you know what they are like, they will all get in a corner and ignore us for the rest of the evening."

   She is a past master at these parties, making sure everyone is talking to someone interesting, and moving people around so no-one gets bored.   Over the years I have become used to making up numbers when needed, and David calls me Rent-a-guest, but it is such fun to dress up for dinner, and just for a little while to enjoy the glamorous life.   I have enlarged my wardrobe to include some ball gowns from the charity shop, encouraged by Dame Barbara, who thinks it's a splendid idea.   When I first confessed that this was where I was getting my dresses from she reminded me that during the war when clothes were on coupons she had started a "library" of beautiful wedding dresses collected from her wealthy friends.   These were for women in the armed forces to borrow so they could have a romantic wedding.   She was awarded a Certificate of Merit by Eastern Command.

   She has always encouraged thrift.   When a young girl starting to be asked to smart balls and dances there was no money in her family to spare for ball gowns.   Her grandfather had lost the family money and had shot himself, and her father had been killed in the last year of the Great War.   Her mother had to struggle to bring up her two sons and Dame Barbara.   Dame Barbara started to write a society column for the Daily Express to earn some money and overcame the problem of gowns by borrowing dresses from a young man just starting out in the fashion world called Norman Hartnell.

   She always said that she learnt her journalistic skills from Lord Beaverbrook at the Express, and that this was a great help when she started to write her novels.   It was also a great help when she had to deal with the hundreds of people wanting to come and interview her for newspapers and magazines. She never turned anyone down, however amateur they were, as she said she remembered what it was like when she first started out. But she got very upset at some of the snide remarks and personal comments about her style of dressing that some people wrote and printed, although as she said she felt it was mostly jealousy at her success. "The British hate success, especially successful women." I heard her telling someone on the phone one day that if she only wanted to interview her to send her up not to bother, she could send herself up far better! It got to such a point, especially after her connection with Princess Diana, that she had to insist that anyone who wanted to interview her had to sign a declaration that she could vet the material.

Not many people seem to be aware that she is not only a romantic novelist, but has also written cookery books, plays, poetry and an operetta, to name but a few. Among her campaigns she won the right for gypsies to have permanent camps so that their children could go to school, was instrumental in bringing prayers back into assemblies in schools, and fought for better salaries for midwives and nurses. She is always ready to put up a fight for her convictions, and even in her nineties appeared on television to accuse Jackie Collins of making money from writing what she considered filth which she felt was corrupting the young. She wrote "Love at the Helm" helped by Earl Mountbatten in aid of the Mountbatten Memorial Trust, and fiercely defended the Earl after he died when his handling of the Burma campaign was criticised. As she said, not only was he not alive to defend himself, but to denigrate the campaign was to belittle all the men who had given their lives in Burma, and for the sake of the widows and orphans she felt this must be countered. She is always ready to support the underdog and is more in touch with the world of politics than I am. In fact she had Margaret Thatcher to lunch in an effort to warn her the knives were out just before the Prime Minister was ousted from office. As she said to me "You can't get away with telling men they are fools too often, darling, they never forgive you, and they never forget."

If she dies before me, which I doubt, it won't be just the glamorous parties I shall miss but the talks we have about every subject under the sun. She likes me to call in for a chat about 10 a.m., before she gets up to start another hectic day. By then she has sorted out her engagements for the day with one of her secretaries, arranged the meals with the chef, and given instructions to the chauffeur. Her maid has been told what dresses to lay out, she has seen some of the more urgent letters and had the major news items read to her from a collection of daily papers. Her eyes are beginning to fail which she finds very trying, but if that is all that's wrong with me when I am in my late 90's I shall not grumble.

We put the world to rights, and I hear tales of the rich and famous, but quite often our talk is interrupted by the telephone. Sometimes she has been booked to give an interview over the phone with radio stations in America and Australia at this time of the day. It amazes me the information and opinions she can pack into a three-minute slot, but I sometimes feel sorry for the interviewer trying to get a word in edgeways. At times I have the same trouble, but she always asks after David and the family, and gives me some fairly firm advice on how to keep them in line.

Her maid runs her bath on the dot of 10.45, and with the water cooling we reluctantly have to part with promises to call again soon. "And don't leave it so long next time, darling." As she says, most of her friends her age are "either dead or gaga", so I think she really enjoys my friendship as much as I enjoy hers.

With a strong Christian faith she is certainly not afraid of dying, updates her obituary regularly, and is very keen to make sure her funeral is carried out just as she would want it. I was asked to call in at our local undertakers to check on the prices of a marble angel. "Don't say it is for me, as I am sure the last lot of undertakers I asked gave me an inflated price when they knew who it was for." Of course, I am well known as David's wife in the local funeral director's and the lovely lady in there said, when asked to quote for an angel, "I would have thought you were more of a squirrel or rabbit person!"

ADDENDUM:

Since writing this my dear friend has died, just a few weeks short of her 99th birthday. She had no fear of death only its manner - "I don't want to be dribbly" she said - and in the end nature was kind. Suddenly age caught up with her, and over the last few weeks of her life she gradually slipped away, giving those of us who loved her time to come to terms with life without her.

She had thought carefully about her funeral, planning it down to the last detail, and it was as perfect as she would have wished. She died peacefully in her own bed, surrounded by her family. Three days later, on a summer's morning, we assembled, to follow her cardboard coffin from the house, up the path lined with flowers in all shades of pink, some large and ornate, lilies and orchids next to bunches of wild flowers. As she had requested, immediately behind the family walked her staff, her chef, her gardener, secretaries and carers. Then the rest of us, Lords, Princes, Counts and Countesses, friends and neighbours, local shopkeepers. The women were elegant in black with touches of white, hats large and small, flowered and frilled, jewellery sparkling in the sun.

Across the grass we walked in silence, the lake gleaming in the distance, the rhododendrons and azaleas great splashes of colour, the chestnut trees in full flower. We gathered under the Elizabethan Oak, said to have been planted by Elizabeth 1 on the spot where she killed her first stag.

The canopy of the great oak formed a pale green ceiling above as the coffin was lowered gently into the grave. The service was simple and short. Her daughter Raine read a passage from St. John's letters reminding us of the love we should have for each other and the whole world of nature. Her grandson William recited a poem written by Dame Barbara some time ago, then a few words of comfort from the Vicar, a few prayers. No pomp and ceremony, no choir, organ, massed priests and bishops in a great cathedral, just the sun glinting through the leaves and the sound of bird song.

Her two sons, who loved their mother dearly, had worked hard to carry out her wishes for her funeral, and led the slow file of people past the grave, each person stooping to sprinkle a handful of soil onto the coffin.

Back in the house the rooms felt empty though full of people sitting quietly with their own memories. I could not help feeling that any moment Barbara would bustle through the door, in her usual cloud of pink, and I would hear her voice "Now then darling, don't be feeble, cheer up!".

Time to leave Camfield, the sun had gone, clouds had gathered, and as we walked to the car rain began to fall.

Chapter 4

A Journey into the Past
* * * * * * * * * *

On the home front the boys were starting at university, and the medical profession were hauling themselves into the 20th century and encouraging the building of custom-built premises for GPs, with full-time receptionists, switch-board operators, nurses and practice managers. I counted at one time 23 part- and full-time staff at David's new Medical Supermarket when it was built, apart from the doctors; these replacing the five wives and three receptionists! This meant I had more free time, which was just as well as a new challenge came along which I could not resist.

I should have known better, but like all get-rich-quick schemes it sounded so easy, and anyway, David said it would never work, which as all sensible husbands know is fighting talk. A group of business men wanted to start up an upmarket tour of Hertfordshire, complete with luxury coach, champagne lunch on board, an English tea taken at some country house and finishing up with an Elizabethan banquet at one of our stately homes. All I had to do was work out a suitable tour, taking in as many varied places of interest as possible. Hertfordshire has so many known and unknown places to visit the difficulty lay in what to leave out.

The first meeting was great. I was invited to become a director of the company for a "small contribution", the size of which would be reflected in my share of the profits. I knew I would be pushing my luck to ask David for any money, but I creamed off so much of the housekeeping that even David began to wonder if we were not taking our new healthy high-fibre diet of baked beans a little too far.

In the meantime the meetings went on, and it soon became apparent, to me anyway, that it was not going to be the plain sailing it had been made out to be. Problems began to arise on all sides, and a whole new world hedged round with regulations and a positive mine field of paper work opened up. Apparently you must apply for various licences to start up a new tour, and even with one of our consortium in the coach business this was very tricky. It seemed to be a bit like planning permission: you lodged your plans of the tour with full details of the places to be visited, routes to be followed, and timetables, and any interested party, i.e. the police or other tour operators, could lodge objections. The custom was to put in half a dozen different schemes in the hope that one at least would get through. This took me quite a time to work out, and quite a lot of petrol as well.

The next stumbling block appeared at the same time. Although our tour operator was licensed to pick up from any suitable point in Hertfordshire, he was not licensed to go into London and make pick-ups. This tour was aimed at the very top end of the market (it had to be when you worked out the price), and I did not see how you could expect these sort of people to nip on a tube to Cockfosters where we would be waiting in the car park to serve them coffee, even with quality biscuits.

A fleet of Rolls Royces nearly got the vote till someone, not the accountant, pointed out that it would cut our profits in half, so it was finally decided to use minicabs.   The plan was to park the coach at some suitable place, like the forecourt of a large public house or hotel, serve them coffee as they arrived, and let them "freshen up" using the local facilities.   Guess who was sent round to find such a place and to ask for the use of the loos?   Some proprietors were quite polite, really; others I will draw a veil over.   It came down to money of course.   "Use of facilities, let's see, that will be so much, opening up specially out of hours, extra staff, so much.   And no deal unless we get to serve the coffee. Then there's the question of parking for a large coach. As we don't normally take coach trade we shall have to make a charge for that as well."

My job was rapidly expanding in other directions.   As all the men "worked properly", and I just did my little things from home, anything that needed doing during the week fell to me.   This seemed mostly to be finding an endless supply of suitable loos along our proposed route - shades of the Duke of Bedford.   I also had to write out the brochure for the tour, with photographs, and got so carried away it was more like a small novel before I finished.   Quite rightly it was ruthlessly pruned by the rest of the directors, but unfortunately they then sent it off to the printer without letting me have it back to rewrite.   Time had been slipping by and we were getting desperately near the date set for our first tour, so it was left to the printer to run off 10,000 glossy brochures without proof-reading. I am a great believer that if a piece of paper is the customer's introduction to the goods you are trying to sell him then it must be both impressive and perfect. This point I had mistakenly made at a previous meeting, whereupon one of the others took it upon himself to have headed notepaper, visiting cards and invoice books all beautifully printed with the name of our company, directors' names etc., and while he was at it he was talked into 5,000 carrier bags with our name and logo on them. The accountant meanwhile had organised a stop en route to visit a factory of one of his clients who made model cannons which he was hoping our customers would buy, and had already purchased a dozen on our behalf.

I began to realise we were not going to make our fortunes, especially as the final horror dawned on me when I saw the phone number printed on the brochure for bookings was totally incorrect. When I plucked up courage to ring it, it turned out to be a fishmonger in Aberdeen. The printer refused to reprint unless paid again. As he said quite rightly it wasn't his responsibility to proof-read. The date of our first tour was only two weeks away by now, and of course we had no bookings. I left it to the men to tackle the fishmonger in Aberdeen to see if he would refer any callers but meanwhile something drastic had to be done. Paying my three sons a pittance to alter the phone numbers (I left out other alterations otherwise the brochures would have looked as though they had measles), I rallied our fast dwindling get-rich-quick group. As the tour was to be called "Journey into the Past" what about dressing up in historic costume, hiring a suitable vehicle and driving round London handing out the brochures? It was agreed that desperate measures called for desperate remedies, and we decided to give it a whirl the following Saturday.

Arriving at the coach works in full Elizabeth I outfit, curly red wig, stiff lace ruff, nearly bare bosom and long skirt, I found only two of the others had had the decency to turn up. One was dressed as a pirate as he still had his costume from the last Amateur Operatic Society's rendering of "The Pirates of Penzance". I hadn't the heart to point out that Hertfordshire was about the furthest county from the sea, and the only pirates who came our way were Danes marauding up a local river way back in the dawn of time. The other one, the coach owner, was dressed in full leathers with goggles and helmet and looked like a cross between Biggles and the Red Baron. The reason for this became only too apparent when he disappeared into the coach works to appear driving an open-backed vintage lorry with what looked like an old-fashioned milk float perched on the back.

In fact it *was* a milk float, festooned with plastic parsley and green grass mats borrowed from the local butcher, with a rickety-looking wooden chair lashed to the middle. He seemed so pleased with the general effect I did not like to tell him what I thought of it as a royal carriage. Having hoisted me aboard the float and eased me into the chair we set off - Biggles in his flying helmet and goggles up front, the pirate hanging on grimly to the back of my chair, and me practising a regal look. With hindsight it was unfortunate we had not worked out a system of communication with our driver. He was out of sight and reach up the front, and quite deaf with his helmet on.

It was also extremely unwise to have taken up our positions with five miles to cover to the centre of London. The roads were fairly clear as it was a Saturday, and gathering speed we hurtled along the A6 with the wind disappearing down my cleavage and threatening to rip my lace ruff off. One hand was needed to hold on to the pearl-bedecked wig and the other to keep me on the chair. The pirate was having troubles of his own. Standing up was quite out of the question and he quickly took up a grovelling position behind my chair and appeared to be praying. Shouting "SLOW DOWN" had no effect, and for once the traffic lights were all green. Bits of plastic parsley and grass blew past in the slip-stream, and the only bright spot was the sight of people's faces in oncoming cars.

We finally drew into a bus lay-by near Euston, at which point the pirate collapsed onto the remains of the lawn, moaning feebly. Biggles appeared, unwrapping himself from layers of woollen scarves and told us to smarten up and get ready to distribute the leaflets. He announced our route would be up Oxford Street, round Marble Arch, back down the other side of Oxford Street to Oxford Circus, down Regent Street to Piccadilly and back up to Oxford Circus again. He promised faithfully to drive slowly and in a stately fashion more in keeping with his royal passenger and her consort. So we set off.

Have you ever noticed how difficult it is to give even bits of paper away to people? I must admit I have hurried past the thrusting hands myself. From a moving vehicle it is well nigh impossible. At the end of the first run we took stock again.

The pirate decided to abandon his eyepatch which cut down his vision too much, because even if there was an outstretched hand, by the time he had noticed it with one eye tear-filled from the wind, and unclenched a hand from one of the milk float uprights, we were well past. From my place on the "throne" I couldn't reach anyway, and the only good spot was round Piccadilly Circus where, because the traffic moved so slowly, we had a limited success. It was decided that we would go round again and that I would cast leaflets with gay abandon and a regal wave of the arm towards any group of likely customers, and that the pirate would hop down when we came to a complete halt at places like traffic lights.

Unfortunately the pirate, bless him, although stout of heart, was also stout of figure, and not in the first flush of youth. He leapt off at the top of Regent Street and started thrusting leaflets into the hands of a group of Japanese who had kindly retrieved him from the pavement and put him back on his feet. Shouting "Gadzooks" and "Have at you, sir", which he considered added a suitable historic flavour to the proceedings, he got quite carried away, and flushed with success willingly posed for the battery of cameras the Japanese produced. At that moment I got carried away as well as the lights changed to green. My regal waves and smiles turned to shouts of anguish as we gathered momentum, urged on from behind by a double-decker bus and a taxi, from both of which came a stream of abuse I am sure no other Queen has had to suffer.

Unable to turn my head because of the ruff I finally caught sight, out of the corner of my eye, of a purple-faced pirate hanging onto a stanchion and making valiant efforts to get a leg over the side. Luckily Biggles up the front saw him in the wing mirror and came to a halt. Traffic behind us was starting to build up the length of Regent Street, so at a hastily-convened directors meeting it was decided discretion was the better part of valour and we would finish the circuit in double quick time and then head for Regents Park for a breather. The speed with which we shot off, coupled with the exercise already experienced by the poor pirate, reduced him to his previous grovelling position at the back of my chair, desperately trying to get out of the slip-stream so he could catch his breath. I realised it was all down to me, and we still had thousands of brochures to get rid of. Grabbing handfuls at a time I cast them into the slip-stream as we hurtled round Marble Arch and down Oxford Street. The wind was unbelievably cold, and cut through the naked portion of my chest between ruff and cleavage till I could stand it no longer. I grabbed the stocking hat off the head of the pirate who by this time had his face buried in my skirt, and thrust it down the front of my dress. I found that by gripping the woollen bobble in my teeth it cut out some of the draught.

As we drew into the Park I became aware of the sound of sirens and wondered where the fire was. We slowed down and the noise rose to a crescendo as down both sides of the milk float came two enormous black police motor-bikes with two huge black leather-clad policemen on them. For a moment, as we all came to a majestic halt, I knew what heads of State and Royalty must feel like. They climbed ponderously off their bikes, growing larger by the minute, and one started a slow prowl round the outside of our lorry, while the other slowly unbuttoned a flap in his jacket and produced a notepad and pen. I swear he did a knees bend and said, "Now then, now then, what's all this then?", but as I was the only person able to see or hear at that moment I have no witnesses. Biggles was struggling to get his helmet off - it had not been used for some years and the buckle had jammed with the strap across his mouth. The pirate, although a slightly better colour from what I could see of him, was beyond speech.

I removed the bobble hat, smiled sweetly, and asked what I could do for him. "It's not what you can do for me," he said, extremely coldly I thought. "It's what I am going to do to you!" He then started ticking off our offences one by one. "Unauthorised distribution of literature in a public place, throwing litter onto the streets of the Metropolis, causing numerous obstructions, soliciting for custom on a public highway." (I didn't like the sound of that one). "Contravening so many bye laws I haven't time to enumerate them, and finally entering a royal park in a commercial vehicle dressed in an unseemly manner." (I hastily tried to replace the bobble hat). "And I am sure," he continued, "I could find quite a few more without trying too hard, while my friend here," waving a hand towards the other large figure, "will fill you in on all the laws you have broken or disregarded concerning this lot," he said, waving a disdainful hand at our equipage.

At this point, whether it was the fact that I was so cold, bruised and battered, or I had finally admitted to myself that our business venture was a complete washout, somehow the whole bitter disappointment of it all welled up inside me. I am ashamed to admit I burst into tears. "I've had enough," I cried. "Just let me go home, I'll never do it again". "Oh my gawd," said the second copper. "Get them out of here quick". By this time we were starting to gather a crowd, and the sight of Queen Elizabeth I snivelling into a woollen hat, apparently being bullied by two large policeman, was beginning to raise partisan feelings among the onlookers. At this point Biggles managed to snap the strap of his helmet and rushed round the side of the lorry, promising to drive straight back home and never darken their patch again.

"You've got a couple of minutes to vanish while

our backs are turned," growled PC No. 1. "When I look round I don't even want to know you ever existed." "And get 'em off the back of that monstrosity before you go," added the other one. In a way it was lucky it was in the days before seat belts, as we managed to wedge the pirate between us in the cab, and headed for home.

The emergency meeting of all directors and accountant was held at the bedside of the pirate a few days later, when his wife finally let us in to see him. Deciding, in view of his frail state, to keep the accusations and recriminations between us to a minimum, we wound up the venture. Not before the coach owner had slapped in a bill for use of the milk float and lorry, and the accountant a hasty bill for work so far and "sundries", which all nicely took care of any remaining money in the kitty. David restrained himself from saying "I told you so" - which was just as well.

Chapter 5

Goodnight, Sorry for Sinking You
* * * * * * * * * *

On November 6th, every year since I have known him, David telephones his two brothers and his sister. I knew this was the anniversary of the sinking of the SS City of Cairo, torpedoed by a U-boat on this date in 1942 in the South Atlantic. I also knew that David, then aged twelve, was on board with his two elder brothers and his sister. Their mother had decided to brave the trip home from India with the children for the sake of their education. David's father, who was in the Indian Civil Service, remained behind.

Those of us old enough to remember the second World War, even as small children, each have very different memories. Mine, as a child of five when the war broke out, revolved round the mysterious disappearance of bananas, the lack of elastic to mend my doll, and the sudden inability to go on the beach (we lived in Hastings), owing to the erection of vast quantities of barbed wire between me and the sand and sea. My war wounds consisted of taking too literally the primary school head mistress's demand that we fall to the floor when we heard the siren, or when she blew her whistle, and being heavily bruised every time my grandmother hauled me out of bed in the night raids, dragging me down two flights of stairs to the cellar.

Having a very sweet tooth I also suffered greatly from the sweet rationing. Carrying a small tin of emergency rations at all times in case I was buried under the rubble of a building became more and more difficult, as I knew that among other goodies in the tin half-a-dozen barley sugars had been sealed into it. I put down the fact that I am unable to diet for any length of time to the awful trauma I suffered when I was finally allowed to open it at the end of the war to find that small beetle-like insects had taken up residence and reduced the contents to a powder. However, as I was to find out, David's wartime experiences were very different, although one of the effects was similar, as it explained his capacity to eat like a horse when the opportunity arose.

I might still never have heard the full story of what happened to David, his family, and other passengers and crew of the ship the City of Cairo if it were not for the interest taken by a journalist and author called Ralph Barker. He had always been particularly keen on stories of courage and endurance, and during the course of his researches came across some newspaper accounts of the sinking of this ship, written in 1943, by some of the survivors, including David's mother May. Intrigued, he began to uncover more and more first-hand accounts of what happened to the various survivors, and then began to trace any people who might still be alive. The result was a book called "Goodnight, Sorry for Sinking You" published in 1984 by Collins, and for the remaining survivors an extraordinary re-union that year on board HMS Belfast moored on the Thames. This re-union included Captain Karl-Friedrich Merten, the U-boat commander who had sunk them.

The City of Cairo, small at 8,000 tons and too slow to join a fast convoy, was considered fast enough to try it across the South Atlantic alone. It had an uneventful journey from Bombay to Cape Town, and after a few days' break the ship set sail at six on Sunday morning 1st November 1942 bound for Recife. A zigzag course to avoid U-boats extended the distance to over 4,000 miles of open sea from the coast of Africa to the Coast of South America. The only spot of land they would pass would be in the middle of the Atlantic, the tiny island of St Helena, 500 miles north of their expected route.

There were just under 300 people on board, including 44 women and children. There were eight lifeboats, six of 27 feet with a top capacity of 48 at a squeeze, and two other much smaller boats which could each carry 25. On the night of November 6th the children had all gone to bed after an early dinner. The adults, having eaten later, were settling down to various pursuits, chess, bridge, pontoon or chatting over drinks in the saloon. At 8.30 p.m., U-boat 68, commanded by Captain Merten, fired a single torpedo which struck the ship on the starboard side. The lights failed and the ship was plunged in darkness.

People hurried as best they could to get to their lifeboat stations, and mothers tried to go against the flow down to the cabins to fetch their children, and if possible some warm clothing, as most of them were in flimsy evening dresses. David's mother collected her daughter and three sons, made sure they had their life jackets over their pyjamas, and put hers on over her evening dress. She then took them to their boat station, only to find to her horror their boat, Boat 2, had already been launched. In the haste to launch it no-one had put the plug in, and the boat had flooded and tipped up. She hurried them on to the next boat, Boat 4, one of the smaller boats, but was told there was no room.

Refusing to panic she finally managed to get her brood into Boat 3, already over-crowded. Somehow or other seven out of the eight boats were launched, although Boats 1 and 3 were still right alongside the sinking ship.

Meanwhile, Captain Merten, watching the effects of his torpedo, was surprised to see the sinking ship apparently righting itself. His wireless operator reported that the City of Cairo was sending out an SOS on the international distress frequency. Nervous that this message might be picked up by some Allied ship and would put his U-boat in danger, he had the operator intercept the message, using the call-sign of the coastal radio station at Walvis Bay, on the coast of Africa. In this way he stopped any more distress calls, but learnt that the ship was not in fact a troop-ship, but carrying passengers, including women and children. This did not stop him from putting another torpedo into the side of the ship when it showed no sign of sinking.

A column of water three times the height of the ship rose up, together with a shower of debris, to land on most of the boats, but worst damaged was Boat 3, with David and his family in it. This was blown to splinters, and they were all sucked down and down into the sea. Eventually his mother May surfaced, followed by his two brothers and his sister, but no sign of David. May decided she must try and get the children she had found as far as possible from the ship as it sank, so she set off with them into the darkness. Luckily for David, and for me, they bumped into him a short way out. According to him they were the ones who were lost, he knew where he was.

Struggling to keep her children together, May swam through the wreckage trying to reach a boat which had room to take them. But, left with only six boats, mostly waterlogged by this time, and one a small one, she could not find any room. There were still many people in the water trying to find a place in the boats or clinging onto the sides, threatening to capsize them. Eventually Boat 4 took in David and his brother, and Boat 8 took in his other brother, sister and mother.

It was about this time that the U-boat surfaced, and to the horrified survivors looked as though it was training a gun on them. Captain Merten decided they posed no risk, and gave them an approximate position to the nearest land which was St Helena, 500 miles north-north-east, otherwise they were 1,250 miles away from Walvis Bay on the coast of Africa, and about 2,250 miles from Brazil. Deciding he had spent enough time on the surface, he said "Goodnight, sorry for sinking you" and left them to it.

After the U-boat vanished into the darkness there was an eerie silence, then with a hiss and a sigh the City of Cairo slipped under, nearly capsizing some of the remaining lifeboats. Dawn brought a desolate sight: six small boats rose and fell among the wreckage, overloaded and waterlogged, scattered over half a mile of sea. May always remembered that first night with particular horror. An aristocratic lady, she had been brought up with a strict code of etiquette and a rigid standard of behaviour. These attributes were to cause me considerable grief as her daughter-in-law, but her stiff upper lip and refusal to give an inch were to stand her children in good stead in the days ahead, and they probably owed their lives to it.

During that first night, clad only in her evening dress and pearls, she became desperate to go to the lavatory, and had to suffer the indignity in a crowded boat of being held over the side. With daylight the boats started to head towards each other. Each boat had oars, but they were extremely heavy, and difficult to use in the crowded conditions. Most of the male passengers were elderly or unfit for military service, but they finally managed to get close enough for the officers to count heads. Only six men were missing, which seemed a miracle in view of the chaos and confusion.

Views differed as to what their best course of action should be. Some of the passengers thought they should try to remain where they were as they all believed their SOS had been answered, and that a plane or ship would be arriving at any minute. In fact it was to be a week before the Cairo was reported overdue, and then of course no one knew where to look.

The Captain felt their only hope of survival depended on getting to St Helena, which was a British possession, and the only dot of land for over a thousand miles in all directions. But dot it was, only ten by six miles. All the boats had a compass of a sort, but only one had a sextant for taking a fix to steer by, so it was decided to put up make-shift sails to catch any wind, and to row as much as possible during the day, making a rendezvous before dark to keep together. The Captain calculated they would need 21 days to reach land, and the food and drink available would have to be rationed with this in mind. The boats held a fairly plentiful supply of concentrated food, but fresh water was in very short supply. One pint a day, or 20 fluid ounces, was the minimum ration in the tropics to support life, but with the limited amount available and the large number of extra people this would only last a week. In the end it was decided a ration of four ozs a day would have to be sufficient. An effort was made to move people from one boat to another to keep families together, but David and his brother had struck up a friendship with a young woman, Margaret Gordon. Her husband had died in the explosion, and it helped her to come to terms with her grief to entertain the two boys, so they stayed in her boat.

This could have had disastrous consequences, though. The next two days were spent trying to move the boats through the water with the heavy oars towards St Helena, and to cope with the lack of room. With nearly 10 extra people above the normal capacity there was not more than a few inches of freeboard to spare, much less any room to lie down or stretch out. The adults in particular were finding it difficult to come to terms with what might happen to them. The boats shipped water at the slightest movement and with so many bodies crammed together it was difficult to bale.

At first people were not all that hungry. The rations provided in lifeboats at that time consisted of pemmican, hard biscuits, and Horlicks tablets. All very nutritious, but with only 4 ozs of water a day this food quickly became almost impossible to eat. Because of such problems, future lifeboats were to be equipped with different rations, and more emphasis was put on finding ways to increase the supply of fresh water. The sun was also a problem, especially for David, who had skin that burnt easily.

At night the boats tied up together, and people tried to sleep propped up against each other, sharing what little spare clothing they had against the cold of the night. On the third night the wind got up and so did the sea. Boat 4, the smallest, was in great danger of being swamped, and to May's relief David and his brother were passed over into Boat 8 to rejoin the family.

It was becoming apparent by this time that some

of the boats could make better speed than others. Boat 7, for instance, had no rudder and was being steered with an oar. Boat 1 was convinced they stood a better chance of striking out alone, especially because, although the boats had travelled around 50 miles a day, it was in a crab-like fashion, and they were in fact only 10 miles nearer the island.

The fourth night brought an increasing sea, and the first death in David's boat. In the middle of the night an elderly man stood up and tried to urinate over the side, but, stiff and cramped, he lost his balance and under the horrified gaze of David and the rest of the children fell overboard. He drifted past the long line of boats but out of reach, and the Captain shouted that untying any of the boats in the heavy seas and darkness would be madness. David's sister, aged 10, remembers the moment clearly, although she says it did not worry her at the time. However, perhaps it was the thought of being eaten alive by sharks that gave her nightmares in later life.

Next day, day five, the squalls got worse, and the boats more difficult to control. In the end the Captain, against his better judgement, agreed Boat 1 could try and make St Helena to get help, but he still felt it was foolhardy with only a compass. The option was given to the 51 men and three women to move to another boat if they wished, but no-one took up the offer, and before nightfall Boat 1 had disappeared from view.

During the next few days some of the injured and elderly became perceptibly weaker, and one man went insane and tried to throw himself overboard. Someone had to bale day and night in each boat as the waves mounted and it became more and more difficult to remain tied together at night.   Arguments about the water ration broke out, and tempers ran short.   Some people started to drink small amounts of sea water, and on day six there was another death.   In the evening an Indian seaman died who had been drinking sea water, and the following day another Indian was found dead. On the morning of Friday November 13th Boat 6 was missing.   Again the remaining four boats were forced to press on.   Boat 4 got left far behind and by night fall had lost touch with the other three boats.

During the night the mast in David's boat which had been cracked in the launching finally gave way and fell with a crash across the spine of a luckless crew member.   After coping with the wreckage of the mast and sail a space had to be cleared to lay the man flat, adding greatly to the discomfort of the others in the boat.   Next morning Boats 4 and 8 were within sight of each other, out of sight were Boats 5 and 7.   People still hoped that their SOS had been picked up or Boat 1 was nearing help.   More deaths followed but somehow the children remained fitter than the adults and could still be cheered by playing games like "I Spy".   When David's sister asked her mother whether they were going to die too, she replied "Certainly not!", in such a definite tone of voice David said they would not have dared to do so even if they had wanted to.   Anyway, as far as they were concerned only adults died, but as more people died and were thrown overboard it began to have its effect on them.   May was particularly concerned about the Indians in the boats.   Having lived in India for some years she was only too aware of their ability to withdraw into themselves and "will their own deaths".

In some boats the youngest children, little more than babies, caused irritation and distress by their constant crying, louder and more ear-splitting when the tiny ration of water was dispensed. Dr Quantrill, the young ship's doctor, had resisted the temptation to increase the ration to any of the children as he reasoned they were so much smaller they were already receiving more per weight than the adults. In the days when the boats were all still together this young man, fresh from medical school and the delights of a cruise ship, struggled to cope with extremely limited medical equipment and inadequate medicines in circumstances for which his training had certainly not prepared him. I think it was his example that influenced David's decision from an early age to become a doctor. Meeting him at the re-union in 1984, Dr Quantrill said looking back he shudders at the remembrance of his lack of experience, but certainly quite a few of the survivors owe their lives to him. David and I have enjoyed some interesting and hospitable Cowes Week weekends on the Isle of Wight at his home overlooking the finishing line of the various yacht races. He has a fund of fascinating stories of his life since the war.

With the broken mast, Boat 8 with David and family was eventually left far behind and out of sight of any other boat, still 200 miles short of St Helena. As day 13 dawned the officer in charge was so worried at the state of exhaustion and emaciation of his boat-load of humanity he decided to issue the water ration early. By now they were all suffering from swollen limbs, blistered skin and scabs on the face and lips from the sun, and festering sores from the salt water and the inability to move. The night before they had prayed all together for deliverance, and when a ship was sighted just after eight o'clock the next morning May put it down to God having heard their prayers. When she told me this I had an irreverent thought that there would have been big trouble for God if He had not listened.

The children were madly excited and started clambering over the adults to get a better look. In fact it was the sight of these children through the binoculars that caused the Captain of the 8,500-ton Bendoran to throw caution to the wind and steer towards them. He had been nervous in case the boat was a decoy as he had received warnings of U-boats in the area and had just decided to turn away. Somehow they were all hauled on board, but most of them had to be carried to bunks provided for them, and there was another death the following day.

When they were picked up they were still 200 miles short of St Helena, but the Bendoran was sailing for Cape Town, so back they went. The distance they had struggled so hard to cover in the previous 14 days took them just one day. A week later they were back in Cape Town, where David remembers the kindness of people who gave them clothes and shelter until they set sail again six weeks later for Britain.

I wonder what thoughts must have passed through May's mind as she faced yet another danger-fraught trip with her four children, this time in the MS Straat Sunda, a small ship which usually plied between Java and Sumatra. However, at least this time they were travelling in a convoy, and the only real danger they encountered was in the Bay of Biscay. They were caught in the most terrific storm the sailors had ever experienced, the cargo broke loose along with most of the furniture and fittings in the state rooms, and David says it was the only time he began to wonder if they would reach land. But reach it they did, and then David and his brothers and sister were sent straight to school.

All of the survivors of Boat 8 eventually made their way safely to Britain, but what of the other five boats? Boat 1, last seen heading for St Helena with such optimism and carrying the hopes of all the other boats, ran into difficulties almost immediately. Several who had been injured in the torpedo attack died, and even one or two of the fittest died too. By the 15th day half their number were dead. By the 19th day it began to dawn on them they had missed St Helena. After 21 days only eight were left of the original 54 on the boat, and they were down to the last few pints of water. At the end of the fourth week only five were left, two of them so weak they knew death was inevitable. In deference to the increasing weakness of the three remaining survivors they wedged themselves as near the edge of the boat as possible to cause the least effort in heaving them overboard when they died.

Thirty days out, the two remaining men and one young woman were barely alive when it rained. Unable to do more than exist, without the strength to row or set sail, the few pints of fresh water they collected gave them the chance of surviving a few more days. On the 36th day they were sighted by what they thought was a Dutch ship, but in fact it was German. They had travelled 500 miles past St Helena. Their paths with the German ship had only crossed because it had stopped for a few hours the day before with engine trouble, and was on its way from Japan to Bordeaux with a cargo valued at six million marks for the war effort. Obviously a prime target for the Allies.

The two men made a fairly rapid recovery, but unfortunately the young woman had to undergo an emergency operation, and despite the best care her heart was not strong enough and she died. On New Year's

Day, as it approached Bordeaux, the German ship came under heavy attack by Wellington bombers, and was finally sunk by a British cruiser. The German crew got away in four lifeboats, including the two survivors from the City of Cairo. One survivor was in a boat which made for Spain. From there he was sent by train to Madrid, then to Gibraltar and then to England, where he died aged 76 in 1981. The other survivor was picked up by a U-boat, and after being depth-charged and damaged by the RAF the U-boat docked at St Nazaire and he was interned as a POW in Germany till the end of the war.

Boat 6 was spotted by a ship early on the morning of the 14th day with only 50 miles to go to St Helena, and all were taken on board. A few hours later the ship caught up with Boats 5 and 7, within sight of the island. Of the original 166 in these three boats, 150 had survived but a further four died in hospital on the island. Somehow the small island coped with the influx of so many people in need, and Dr Quantrill never forgot their kindness. In 1982 he returned to St Helena as a locum and met many of the islanders who had given so much.

So what happened to the smallest boat, Boat 4, the one David and his brother had hoped to stay in with their new friend Margaret Gordon? As the only woman among 16 men she set herself the task of making them as comfortable as possible by washing bits of their clothing, making sun hats out of a bit of sail, and massaging their legs with oil. But she could not prevent the Indians from drinking sea water. Just a few mouthfuls to start with, but then they could not stop, and after a few days they became delirious. On the day that the survivors from Boats 5, 6 and 7 reached St Helena and safety, the Indians started to die. By day 16, Boat 4 should have been within sight of St Helena themselves, but there was no sign. A few days later there was only one Indian left alive, and after another day without sight of the island he removed his life jacket and threw himself overboard. The remaining survivors decided to stop searching for the island, and with a compass and watch but no sextant they decided to turn west for South America, 1,500 miles away. By the 23rd day there had been two more deaths. Six days later another death reduced the numbers to Margaret and three men. Although the boat, unlike the others, was little more than a rowing boat, with the reduction in numbers at least the remaining survivors were able to stretch out when they were not trying to steer it. By this time the bit of sail they had left was nailed to an oar, and they were also having to bale regularly. Two of the men became weaker and weaker, and finally died within two days of each other.

Now just Margaret Gordon and James Whyte, the third officer of the City of Cairo, were left. As far as he could judge they were 200 miles short of the Brazilian coast, and with perhaps seven days of water remaining. Christmas Day came and went, but at last on December 27th the first rain for 51 days fell, and they collected enough water to increase their chance of staying alive for a few more days. Unknown to them they were only 80 miles off the coast, and later that day were spotted by a Brazilian Navy ship which picked them up. They had travelled 2,000 miles. After spending some time in hospital in Recife, James Whyte was flown to New York, and then joined a ship leaving for Liverpool. Somewhere between New York and Liverpool this ship was sunk with all on board.

Margaret Gordon recovered enough to join the WRNS, and after the war returned to her native Australia. It was not until Ralph Barker, becoming more and more intrigued with the various twists and turns of the fate of the lifeboats, managed to trace and contact Margaret, and then contacted David and his family that David knew she was still alive. At the re-union on HMS Belfast in 1984, after the publication of Ralph Barker's book, David had hoped she would be there, but unfortunately she had decided not to make the journey from Australia; like quite a few of the survivors her memories were too painful. David's memories of her and her cheerful kindness in those first days after the sinking led him to write to her, and eventually she surprised him by coming to stay with us for a couple of days when she was over from Australia on a tour of Britain with a gardening club. Although then in her seventies she was still a capable, energetic woman, full of enthusiasm for life, and I could see how David and his brother must have wanted to stay with her in Boat 4, but I am sure they would not have survived those 51 days.

On the Belfast I met Captain Merten, who had been in correspondence with Ralph Barker, anxious to set the record straight about his part in the sinking. The night before he had dined with the remaining officers from the City of Cairo, and when they were asked on Breakfast TV what were their feelings the officers said it was the duty of all sailors in wartime to sink as much enemy shipping as possible, but behind it all there was still the fellowship of the sea. Captain Merten himself, a ramrod figure even at 80, asked me who I was. I told him I was no-one important, only a wife of one of the survivors. "Madam," he said with a click of his heels,

"No lady is unimportant." I am afraid this did not alter my opinion. Sinking the ship was his job, but, as far as I was concerned, to intercept that SOS to stop it being heard went beyond the call of duty.

If it had not been for the book "Goodnight, Sorry for Sinking You", and the re-union, I doubt whether I would ever have understood why it is so important to David to ring round his family on November 6th, and it gave me a better understanding of his attitude to holidays and life in general!

Chapter 6

David's Idea of a Holiday
* * * * * * * * *

The effect of David's experiences seemed to be that he was immune from any form of physical discomfort, or it could have been something to do with many years at boarding school. Whatever it was, as long as he had food at regular intervals nothing else seemed to faze him. We married on £75, my £75, as David was penniless after six years at medical school, followed by a couple of house jobs. For these he was at least paid the princely sum of £600 per year. House jobs at hospital lasted six months and no time off. He asked for an afternoon off to go to his brother's wedding and was told he was welcome to go, but not to return, or expect another job. After finishing his house jobs he then did his compulsory National Service, and as an army doctor was paid the equivalent of £1.25p a day.

He enjoyed his National Service as he ended up in Japan, having volunteered for Korea, being one of the few unmarried doctors available at that time. He was sent off by sea, and by the time he reached Korea the war had ended and he was sent on to Japan. The base hospital was there, but as the war had finished he found himself rather surplus to requirements and ended up teaching soldiers to ski.

Never having ski-ed before it was a case of the blind leading the blind, but it stood him in good stead in later life when our smart friends started comparing ski-ing stories and where the best pistes were. While in

Japan he again escaped a brush with death in the sea. He went sailing off the small islands with the adjutant to the General and they capsized. Luckily, as he was sailing with such an important person, a search party was organised when they did not return after some hours, and they were finally picked up eight hours later by Japanese fishermen. The adjutant spent some days in hospital, but David with his reddish colouring, and after his lifeboat experiences, always swam or sailed in long trousers and a long-sleeved shirt if he was in warmer climes, and yet again was none the worse for his adventure. Since then he has had one or two more close shaves, and has made his mind up the sea does not want him, which gives me much pain and grief as he will swim almost out of sight when we are at the seaside.

The job he took when we got married paid him £1,000 as an assistant GP for two years, less expenses including the rented accommodation we had to live in. When he was finally made a partner his salary did not increase very much as he then had to pay in for his share of the premises, and it was some considerable time before he reached full parity. After his assistantship was over we could at least look for a house, but were forced to buy a brand new one as it was the only way we could get a 100% mortgage, the bank and building society in those days still being under the impression that doctors were credit-worthy. The mortgage kept us impoverished for many years but it turned out to be a blessing in disguise as house prices rose, especially newer houses. David was also determined he would never undertake to have any private patients, as he felt very strongly the only thing a private patient should pay for is time, the treatment should be the same for both

National Health patients and private. Having a full list of National Health patients he was not prepared to give up the time they should have for private patients. Over the years I have had to put this point of view to quite a few people who have rung me up and tried to get me to persuade David to take them on "at any price". For a start I point out that I am the wrong person to ask, extra patients mean extra time away from me and from the family. It is very difficult to be jealous of ill people and not feel guilty, and I think with shame of occasions when I got very upset when David, although not officially on duty, would go to visit someone sick or in distress.

One such time was the day of our youngest son's christening. David's formidable mother and a large contingent of his family were coming for lunch and tea. I specially wanted the house to look nice, the two older boys to look smart, the baby beautiful and the food to be good. David had promised me his undivided help and attention for the whole day but as he was cutting the lawn the telephone rang. The operator said she knew he was not on duty and his telephone was switched but she had a very distressed lady on the phone wanting David and only David. All I could make out was that she was just back from holiday and needed the doctor urgently. I tried giving her the name and telephone number of the doctor on duty, but it was no use, and in the end I had to reluctantly call David. I went out to stop my eldest from mowing over his sibling who was busy throwing grass everywhere when, to my horror, I heard David's car start up and zoom off down the road.

For the next couple of hours, as I coped with a crying baby and two over excited and grass-stained boys while trying to prepare all the food and hoover the house, my thoughts were extremely uncharitable. David got back half-way through lunch, and it was not till late evening that I had a chance to vent my frustration and fury at him for not putting me first for once. Imagine my horror when he told me the woman who had rung had indeed just got back from a holiday at the seaside where, the day before, she had seen her seven-year-old son, who David had delivered, drown. And I had spent the day thinking how selfish *she* was. No wonder that I have often thought, over the years, it might have been easier to cope with a blonde rather than 15,000 patients.

I had always longed to travel, something that David of course had done as a child commuting to India, and then as a student and in the army. I had a couple of weeks on a school trip to France and that was it. For our honeymoon we had five days in a B & B in Devon, with the promise of an exotic holiday abroad when we could afford it. Thirty-seven years later, and Patagonia was certainly exotic, not least when the ground opened under him and David fell into a sewer, luckily managing to catch hold of the edge before he vanished 10 feet down into murky brown sludge. Patagonia is not the sort of place where you attempt to get compensation from the local council, but at least I was able to dump the clothes he was wearing. If it had happened on our more recent trip to Costa Rica, Honduras and the Yucatan, I don't know what we would have done. David's suitcase went missing on our flight out, not catching up until we reached home three weeks later. He spent the entire holiday in what he stood up in plus two pairs of socks and two T-shirts provided by the airline. I washed him out every night and pegged him up to dry. The climate was very humid and extremely hot, so he did not appear to notice he was always slightly damp, and as we had 15 flights in 16 days we did not stay long enough for anyone to realise he did not have much of a change of clothes.

By the time we got back he had decided travelling light was for him, and it was just not necessary to take so much, which was unfortunate when we went on our next holiday to Madeira and stayed in a smart hotel for a week. It was so smart that when we went up to the restaurant for dinner the first night we were turned away because David was not wearing a tie. Having borrowed a tie from someone in the same party, the next night we were turned away because of his trainers, even though they were designer ones and fairly new. Fed up by this time with the thought of eating all our meals in the basement coffee shop I took him down town and bought him a tie, a long-sleeved white shirt and a pair of brown shoes. I presented him for inspection and luckily for all concerned he passed.

In the beginning, when our three boys were old enough to want to have holidays, I was talked into going camping. Never having been, or wanted to be, a Girl Guide I had a feeling I was not outward bound material. I have never had anything against a five star hotel, something which I still cannot get David to agree to, especially after his brush with the one on Madeira. But the camping idea sounded reasonable enough. We were to go with two friends who were keen campers, a professor of biochemistry and his wife, and their two children. They suggested we hired a tent and equipment to see if we liked it before laying out a lot of money on our own tent. I was still reluctant till it was decided we would go to Brittany for our trial run. In those days you could take a car from the airfield near

Southampton to Cherbourg on a cargo plane, a very civilised way of travelling.

I had to admit that the holiday was a great success - we had glorious sunshine for 14 days, and the cheapness of the wine helped me to see camp life through a rosy glow. The boys loved every minute, and David and the professor spent their time talking shop together to the exclusion of all else, including mislaying the five children they were supposed to be keeping an eye on. Given a nice safe job like the washing-up they managed to forget to bring it all back from the washing block, and we had to exist with paper plates by the end.

Fired with enthusiasm, we bought a large tent and all the various paraphernalia to go with it for our future holidays. Unfortunately for the next nine years we did not seem to have a dry or warm day during our two weeks. Perhaps we should not have chosen places with names like St Cloud, where the boys and David had to concoct marvellous drainage ditches through the centre of the tent, so I could stand on two bits of cardboard, straddling a ditch of rushing muddy water to cook the meals. That was the holiday the boys ended up with only their pyjamas and track suits dry enough to travel back in. The Prof. and his wife had given up camping the previous year and had invested in a caravan, which David began to bring into the conversation at regular intervals. However, on consulting the Prof's wife I learnt that their first trip had not been much of a success. It was nice to have all mod cons under one roof, and at least it was dry, but they had all gone down with Montezuma's revenge on the last day of their holiday and had omitted to seal down the lid of the lavatory when they drove back to the ferry. The memory, much less the smell, lingered on.

David said we need not go to such lengths as a caravan, a motor van would be just as good. Before I knew it I was the proud owner of a little Austin-Morris camper. I was pleased to have my own vehicle at last, but found considerable difficulty in parking as the wardrobe obscured the view out of the back. Little was the operative word, although I could be the only mum needed to take the school football team to an away match before the days of seat belts. When we gave it a trial run for a weekend away with the three boys the disadvantages began to show up. To show this new way of life off to its best advantage David booked us into a very smart site belonging to the Camping and Caravaning Club of Great Britain.

When we parked on the site allocated to us I was a bit intimidated by the surrounding smart mobile homes and caravans, not helped by our inability to hitch up to all the various supplies and outlets provided for each site, which had been proudly itemised by the man at the reception desk. Our little van was not wired for electricity and had a bucket under the sink/handbasin which was only the size of a pudding basin anyway. It did have a feature which I was very proud of, a small canister which could be filled with water and connected up to a foot pump, this in turn pumped water into the basin, or would have done if someone remembered to reconnect the hose each time the canister was refilled.

The roof pushed up when stationary to give a little more headroom, nearly enough for David to stand upright in the back, that is until the two hammocks were folded down out of the roof for the bigger boys. Underneath these the "sofa" unfolded to take up every remaining inch of floor space in the back as the double bed. The third and smallest boy was to sleep in a hammock which was hung across the front driver and passenger seats. The stove had two gaz burners and a grill, more suitable in size for a doll's house and certainly not big enough to cook enough to satisfy the four men in my life, especially with appetites made even sharper by the bracing sea air. Finally that first night I sent them all off to the toilet block and cleared up. As darkness fell David and the boys fell over each other putting the beds up while I stood outside, the only place not filled with bedding and bodies.

It all seemed a bit dark and eerie, especially as we had no lights in the van. I was used to continental camp sites with lines of lights, but David said he would make sure we were quite secure. This meant him locking the back door of the van and the driver's door from the outside, then climbing in through the passenger door and locking that from the inside. Kneeling on the double bed, he then put the hammock up across the front. Getting undressed and into bed was a bit like one of those rubic cubes, but eventually we all managed it, and peace descended as the boys fell asleep, even the youngest one, who kept complaining bitterly that the steering wheel was taking up all the room in the front. But David kept fidgeting. It then turned out that he had made sure the boys had done a pee at the toilets, but had forgotten to go himself. The only way to get out of the van was through the passenger door, as this was the only one he had locked from the inside, but with the hammock wedged across the front and Edward at last asleep it would have meant doing the rubic cube in reverse once more. Finally David solved it by kneeling on me and peeing out of the little sliding window situated over the stove, not, apparently, what is expected of   Camping and Caravaning Club members, as the lady from the next door site told me icily next morning when I met her in the queue for the bread. It was just lucky she thought it was one of the boys.

Even David had to admit the van was not the answer in the end. We tried taking a small tent as well for two of the boys, but when it rained or when I tried to cook everyone wanted to be "indoors". A few years later we took the boys up to London to the Model Railway Exhibition, but the queue was so long David found a shorter one round the corner which turned out to be the Boat Show. I had a quiet sit down with a cup of coffee while David and the lads went round the stands. A big mistake, this time on my part, almost as big a mistake as David buying me a pottery kiln.

First back was Ed, squeaking with excitement about Dad having bought a boat. Second back were the other two boys, confirming this mad tale. Third back was David looking guilty. With all four of them so excited, and all giving their version of what David had bought, there was a slight misunderstanding on my part. I had had a look round before the coffee, and seen some very nice cabin cruisers which I had foolishly said looked rather super, with dear little kitchens and much more room to move about in. David assured me there would be no problem moving the boat round the country, he would get a small trailer for it, and we could tow it to anywhere we liked. It was apparently a bargain at the price, delivery would be in six weeks, and then "we can start". Foolishly I thought we would be starting on nice little weekends in a nice big cabin cruiser on nice safe rivers or the Broads.

Six weeks later the day of delivery dawned. David went off reluctantly to the surgery and the boys to school. Mid-morning the door bell went. "Sign here

Missus" said the man. "Where is it?" I asked. "All there love," he said, waving his arm to a pile of odd shaped bundles spread over the lawn. "What is that?" I asked. "One boat, for the assembly of ," he said. After a short argument I signed on the understanding that if it was not what was ordered he would return and collect it the next day, but as far as he was concerned there was no mistaking a do-it-yourself Mirror Dinghy as ordered, for a Cabin Cruiser, as expected.

I broke the 11th commandment - thou shalt not ring your husband during surgery unless it is an emergency, and David could not understand why I had not realised it was a DIY boat kit. "We are all going to have such fun building it." I must admit David had endless fun, the boys had quite a lot of fun, and I had no fun at all. For a start, all the bits had to be unpacked and laid out somewhere. Still in a state of shock and outvoted, I had to allow the sitting room to become a cross between a wood-yard and a branch of Homebase. It all took place in a snow storm as the more fragile bits were packed in polystyrene rice crispies.

Years later a pushy vacuum salesman insisted on demonstrating how his machine could suck up dirt I did not know I had got round the edges of the carpet. Not only did he dislodge years of Christmas tree needles, but a vast amount of white rice crispies. He seemed rather surprised I did not want the vacuum, but as I pointed out, having got him to try it on the hall and stairs, I really would not need to clean the edges for a few more years.

As with most new acquisitions the novelty of the boat building wore off fairly quickly for the boys, especially when they had stuck, screwed, or fitted the wrong pieces together while David was still at surgery.

I was lulled asleep on many a night by the sound of
sawing and swearing coming from the garage. Winter
came, and to my horror bits began to migrate from the
garage to our bedroom, something to do with keeping
things at an even temperature. "You'll never notice
them under the bed," said David, "and they are out of
the sight of the boys." However, like Topsy they "just
growed", till getting in and out of bed became an assault
course. Transoms, bilges, centre board, rudder, you
name it, all took shelter under our bed. The centre-
board gave me particular trouble if I had to get up in the
night. The only place for the mast was from the
bathroom, across the landing and into the spare
bedroom.

By spring everything according to David was
"going nicely", although even he could see I was
becoming a little fraught. He suggested I took the boys
away for a weekend while the final assembly took place
and the boat took up its rightful place back in the
garage. "Dave from next door will give me a hand, and
Fred from opposite wants to come over as well. Just
leave us some food and a few beers, and when you
come back it will all be lovely." Unfortunately Fred
and Dave had also told their wives to contribute some
beer. The boys and I came back rather early on the
Sunday afternoon as it had rained most of the day, and
David still maintains that if I had come back later all
would have been well. As I drove down the road
towards our house I could see what looked like the sofa
and two armchairs on the lawn in a steady drizzle.
When I drew up outside not only was the front room
suite outside, but two pelmets and curtains from the
upstairs hall and stair window, and three doors, one
from the bathroom, the sitting room and the kitchen. A

faint sound of singing was coming from the garage, and when I pushed up the garage door, there were Dave, Fred and David sitting on the kitchen stools round the Mirror Dinghy which was resting on our bedspread, propped up by the cushions from the sofa and chairs. Not only had there been an obvious miscalculation about the amount of beer needed to wet the boat, but when David and friends tried to get the various bits of assembled boat down from upstairs they had to do a bit of shunting to and fro, removing and clearing obstacles to the outside as they went.

I am afraid I never took to the boat. We eventually traded the van in for a Mini Traveller, because David had read you could load a Mirror Dinghy on the top, doing away with the need for a trailer. Yes, you can load a Mirror Dinghy on top of a Mini Traveller if your wife is well over 5 feet 4 inches tall, and built like a barn door. With the best will and all the abuse in the world I could not lift my end sufficiently to avoid the danger of scraping either the car or the boat paintwork. That was nothing to the shouting that went on when we actually launched the damn thing in the sea. Perhaps David should not have chosen the North Beach at Salcombe with an onshore wind and heavy sea for a first trial. We got it off the roof and carried it down to the sea, and got it into the waves and out beyond the surf. David then remembered bits of essential equipment like the rudder, oars and life-jackets. Leaving us holding the boat nose into the waves with strict instructions to keep it deep enough not to bump on the bottom he set off for the car-park. By the time he came back the boys had lost interest and gone off to investigate the amusement arcade and I was soaked to the waist. A lot more shouting went on and finally the boys and David were safely into the boat while I continued to hang on to the back. Up went the sail and off went the boat leaving me behind - apparently I should have leapt gracefully over the back as it took off. Not only was I not told that, but I was incapable of leaping anywhere except into a hot bath as I was numb from the waist down by that time. I was to find myself on various expeditions left on shore, on river banks and in car parks, but I have to admit after my one and only outing in the Mirror on a small calm reservoir, that was where I preferred to be. It appears it is not possible to have a ride in a small dinghy without being shouted at, drenched with water, and in danger of being hit with a large lump of wood which swings across one's head at regular intervals, always accompanied with more shouting. The piece of wood is called a boom - after the noise it makes as it strikes one's head!

Chapter 7

Yes, the Earth Did Move
* * * * * * * * *

At last there came a time one summer when the three boys' school or scout trips coincided, and David agreed to a week in Corfu, just the two of us. We stayed in a little concrete apartment block, perched on a precipitous hillside overlooking the sea, just outside the village of Benitses. This holiday started my love affair with the Mediterranean. As David points out, most people are supposed to be descended from primates, but I must have lizard in my blood. I discovered the pleasure of throwing open shutters on a blue sky and sea and a light from the sun that hits your eyeballs like a blow torch. Even better is to get up just before dawn, and watch the sun rise. There is a moment when everything seems to hold its breath, then whoosh, sun's up, day's started, life's awasting. The reluctant pallid light of dawn over a row of wet limp tents in a muddy field does not hold the same magic. Not that I am knocking our green and pleasant land, but it would not be green, as we are discovering, without fairly heavy rainfall.

This first taste of the Mediterranean convinced me it was where I wanted to spend my holidays, but how I achieved this at last was still some way off in the future. In the meantime it was the earthquake on the fifth night that brought in its wake an extra dimension to my cottage industry, a partner, and a totally new line. The five apartments were stacked one on top of each other and consisted of a bedroom, bathroom and small balcony. They had been advertised as B and B, and I wondered when we arrived where we were supposed to have breakfast.

Tired from the travelling and not having caught up with the two-hours-ahead time difference, we were still sleeping peacefully next morning when there was a thunderous bang on the door and a guttural voice bellowed "Breakfast". The door flew back, catching the side of the bed an almighty blow making us both sit bolt upright, and in marched a full-blown Greek brigand with mustachios to match. Slamming a tin tray of china down on the little table in front of the veranda door which he flung open with a crash, he then produced a long loaf from under his arm, slapped that down on the table, and marched back out of the bedroom, eyes flashing and riveted as I realised too late on my skimpy nightie. This scenario was repeated every morning, and however much I tried to be awake and dressed before the door hit the bed I never quite made it.

He seemed to vanish completely after the breakfast delivery and there were no houses near by, but some time during the day when we were out the bed would be made and the tray removed. The breakfast was just right, a pat of creamy butter, a dish of peach jam, and coffee you could stand a spoon in. How I hate these soulless Euro-correct foil wrapped pieces of tasteless butter, and even more the little foil pots of jam with the pretty pictures of fruit on the lids. These pictures are an insult, as you peel back the foil the contents owe nothing much to fruit, but a lot to sugar and colour. The bread was delicious too, rather like a long French baton, but the middle bit I noticed had a slight strange smell which I could not place. David said it was probably some pungent local herb. As I discovered on the last day it was actually pungent Greek armpit. Having made it to the veranda early I saw our breakfast bread arriving, five loaves wedged under the arm of the brigand while he sweated and puffed his way up the steep hill from the village. "I'll have the middle bit." said David happily. "What the eye doesn't see and all that."

We had seen very little of the couples in the other apartments and when we did catch a glimpse in true Brit style we just nodded politely, but the night of the earthquake changed all that. I woke up in the middle of the night to absolute silence. No noise of cicadas, no dogs barking, no cockerels with insomnia, no noise of late night revellers on mopeds, even the sea was silent. At that moment David woke up too. He reached out and turned on the bedside light, and I was just about to say how strange to be woken up by silence when we heard a noise like an underground train coming towards us. As the noise increased the whole block started to vibrate. Everything on the bedside table and dressing table started to shake, rattle and roll, the light went out and the bed started to judder. Stuff started to fall off the dressing table onto the floor, there was a crash as a glass fell. The train roared past and died away, the rattling died down and the shaking stopped. It seemed an eternity, but I suppose it can't have been more than a few seconds. "What on earth was that !" "Only an earthquake," said David. "We had a few in India, but I must admit that was quite a big one." Suddenly damp tents in muddy fields seemed highly attractive.

The light flickered on and we heard people hurrying down the steps at the back. Avoiding the debris on the floor, we decided to join them. Every dog, donkey, cockerel and bird was making its feelings known, and obviously no sleep was going to be possible for the rest of the night as no-one was keen to go back inside, especially as David warned there might be a few aftershocks. Luckily the night was warm and one or two of the men did go back to bring out a bottle or two of wine and brandy purely for medicinal purposes, and quite a party developed. And this was how we met up with a young couple from Kent. They were both designers, working for a high-powered company in London, but Frances wanted to start a family. She was nervous about giving up her job, both for the money and the satisfaction it gave her, but on the strength of a few days away from my boys I gave her a rosy picture of running one's own business from home, conveniently forgetting the perpetual juggling of children, husband and job it entails. We exchanged telephone numbers and the usual promises to keep in touch and that I thought was that.

Five months went by and then there was a telephone call. "This is Frances, I met you in Corfu. I am three months pregnant and have given up work. Now what do I do?". I must admit I felt a bit responsible, as I had laid it on with a trowel about how easy it was to combine motherhood and a job from home. My business was booming, but I found that however well my products sold, each year the shops would ask me if I had anything new. I had exhausted the things I could put pot-pourri in, but felt I still needed something in the soft material line that would be easy to parcel up and send.

An idea that had been on my mind for sometime was a tea-cosy of a particular building which appealed to me, a Queen Anne house, one I visited doing deliveries. There was another house I liked, a little Elizabethan black and white timbered building, which I could also see in my mind's eye as a tea-cosy. The stumbling block was that I could not draw a straight line with a ruler, much less turn a house into a tea-cosy. When I asked Frances if she could manage that sort of thing, she just laughed. "I am a designer, that's what designers are for." Within a week I had the drawings in front of me, a beautiful Queen Anne house, correct down to the last detail, even the widow's walk on the top of the roof, so named it is said from the fact that these houses, designed by Christopher Wren and built first in London, were where the wives of the merchants lived. They used to go up onto the roof and walk round in the little rotunda to look for their husbands' ships coming back up the Thames from their perilous voyages.

I had intended to start with tea-cosies based on a particular stately home, but unlike some of their buccaneering forefathers, today's landed gentry are more concerned with making money from products with a proven track record. Most of them also wanted to keep control of anything associated with their individual houses, and would therefore have to buy up the whole run of cosies, quite a considerable outlay. Forced though we were to produce the first designs for general sale, and dependent on my being able to find enough shops prepared to take them, it proved to be a blessing in disguise. It enabled us to iron out any teething troubles and for me in particular to learn another trade.

Suitable material for screen printing had to be found and in a length long enough for the screen printing process. The designs had to be redrawn for each colour used and a separate screen cut. Using more than three or four colours meant more screens to be cut, and the more times the material was run through the printing process the more it cost. The trick was to use a colour partly over a previous one to get shading, but without loss of detail. Each time the material was run through there was a danger of movement or shrinkage, causing blurring of the finished design. Later on we were to do a parrot cage for Parrots the mail-order business, and although Frances drew a perfect cage, the finely detailed bars were too thin to be reproduced however carefully the material was fed through. The parrot was lost behind what looked like a heavy bar code, not an elegant cage. For quite some time after that the boys' beds all had parrot-cage coverlets.

The final economic length was 100 metres, yielding between 300 to 500 cosies, so it was necessary to get each stage right. At first we bought rolls of polyester wadding and cut the individual house shapes out. At the same time we had to buy rolls of heavy lining and cut these out as well, finally machining the different pieces together.

This meant finding more outworkers. I remember only too well a friend insisting she was clever at that sort of thing, and letting her have enough lengths of the various materials to make up 25 of the Queen Anne houses. When she returned them they were semi-circular. She had machined right across the cupola on the top of all of them as she said she had never seen a tea cosy that was not semi-circular. It was quite a tricky business to machine round the cupola and to push the lining and wadding up into it, but of course that was the whole point. As we added more and more house designs we very quickly had to come up with a better and quicker method which would not lose any of the design in the making up.   Luckily for us, Frances's husband was working in London and found a company that would quilt the wadding onto the printed material. For certain cosies we even had the lining quilted on at the same time, making it much easier to machine up and involving only one cutting process.

Packaging was no problem, it was back to the cardboard header with a history of the house depicted, stapled onto a clear plastic bag.   The biggest difficulty was agreeing on a name for our company.   It was worse than trying to think up names for Frances Worters's baby which was imminent.   I remember being particularly struck with   "Hotpots", which she considered naff, and she liked Columbine which I thought was twee.   In the end David and Richard put their foot down about the length of the telephone calls and both claim they chose the final name, Almond-Worters.

Finally we got it all together, the Queen Anne cosy, a smaller black and white timbered Elizabethan house for a granny cosy, and a tall 16th century London town house for a coffee cosy.   Space was already at a premium in London in those days, and these tall narrow houses had some very fine carved wooden details on them.   Carpenters employed in the docks to work on the wooden galleons turned their skills to these houses when they were laid off, which perhaps explains why some of the old prints of the galleons showing their heavily carved sterns remind me of bay windows.

It was unfortunate that getting all three houses printed and made up coincided with the end of the stately home season.   Although I knew that most of them would probably take a few to try at the start of the next season, usually the week before Easter, having nearly a thousand cosies being made up and delivered to be packed, labelled and stored created a problem. This was exacerbated by Frances being well into the nesting syndrome of all new mothers-to-be; in other words her spare bedroom was full of the unnecessary junk one buys for the first baby. I had managed to juggle husband, practice, boys and ageing mother with a growing cottage industry quite successfully up to that point, but the influx of so many tea-cosies was hard to hide. At first I filled up every available space under the beds and in and on top of the cupboards, but packed in slippery plastic they had a habit of sliding out of control like a miniature avalanche if disurbed. I had to find bigger outlets, not dependent on the tourist trade, and that meant selling to shops, preferably London stores, and trying the export market.

Ignorance is bliss, they say. I went up to London with a carrier bag and three samples of the tea/coffee cosies, a few typed price lists and marched into Selfridges. I was directed hither and thither by horrified sales staff who obviously never had a member of the general public try and sell *them* something, until I was finally told that the person I needed was called a buyer. The word "Buyer" was spoken in such a reverential tone of voice I began to lose what little confidence I had, and the last dregs fled when I finally got to the receptionist in the buyer's department. She not only looked stunned but went quite pale when I said no I had not got an appointment, no I had not been in touch by telephone or letter, and no the buyer had not seen my products, nor as far as I knew, heard of Almond-Worters. Taking pity on me, she said I could leave my products if I liked and perhaps the buyer

would have a look when she had a moment. At least I
was street-wise enough to know that would probably be
the last I saw of the cosies. The growing pile of cosies
at home, and the imminent arrival of an extra mouth to
feed in the Worters household made me press on - how
was I to make contact with the buyer when I could not
make an appointment unless she wanted to see me,
having seen my products which I did not want to leave?

Anxious to get to lunch, the receptionist then let
slip that Miss Culter would of course be "at Torquay"
the following week. Under further pressure she told me
Gift Trade Fairs were held two or three times a year and
this was where producers went to show their goods, and
buyers went to choose what they would stock in the
stores and shops for the coming months. I remembered
that a man who had contacted me in the hope of
becoming my agent had mentioned going to Torquay. I
had not been willing to take up his offer of being my
agent as this meant not only quite a hefty percentage of
profit going to him for any sales he made on my behalf,
but I would not have the control over where the outlets
were. This was something I was always determined to
keep. I felt it was very short-sighted to supply a stately
home, and then get orders for the same goods to be sold
in a shop at their gates, much less two shops close
together. You get bored with seeing the same things in
every outlet, and I was sure it would affect repeat orders
if one's products sat on the shelves. It is not a matter of
concern to an agent who if he floods the market will
then find another product to sell having got his
commission. John, the agent who contacted me, was
always telling me what great opportunities I was
missing, but we had remained good friends, so I rang
him to ask how I could show my three cosies at the

Torquay trade fair.

According to him it was all quite simple. "Just think of it," he said "as being like a craft market, but you don't actually sell anything on the spot. You just put up an attractive display, have plenty of price lists, and stand behind it for 9 - 10 hours a day for five days." The fair was held in different hotels and halls in Torquay, each venue having groups of products of a similar nature. John recommended a hotel on the seafront which would suit my cosies, and after a frantic few days re-arranging the school-runs, filling the freezer and getting a few hundred price lists printed, I caught the train to Torquay. I took with me not only the cosies (two of each) but also an old net curtain from the surgery to put over my table, should I be lucky enough to get one. John had told me just to turn up and try my luck.

What a lot of life is sheer luck. When I arrived at the hotel and saw the organiser he was up to the eyes in problems getting the 150 stands sorted and the exhibitors satisfied. At first he was emphatic about no room and no way could I exhibit what ever it was I had. But persistence paid off, especially when I said my entire exhibit was in my carrier bag, I only needed a small coffee table and a chair, and would £25 do - cash? More to get rid of me following him about, he said if I could find a space where I was no trouble to anyone and could provide my own table and chair I could stay.

I found a nice little spot at the entrance, moved a coffee table out of the lounge where it was doing no one any good, draped the net curtain over it, added a chair from the dining room when no-one was looking, and as the cosies looked a bit lonely acquired a plant from the reception desk display. There were special rates for B

& B for exhibitors and I was grateful to take up the offer. John was right, it was a good nine-hour day, always having to look alert, expectant and ready to be pleasant to anyone who stopped to look at your products, even if it was only to say they did not like the colour, size or presentation, and anyway, who used a tea-cosy these days?

After nine hours of that my legs looked like Nora Batty's and I just wanted to fall into bed. I took a few small orders but certainly not enough to make our fortunes, or even go anywhere near covering our costs. Other stands round me were large and very professionally set up, each one manned by at least two or three people. They ordered coffee mid morning, large lunch trays and drinks were delivered mid day, and tea trays in the afternoon. Not used to either hotel life or that of a jet-set company director, I thought the prices charged for food during the day pretty steep. The inclusive breakfast was very lavish, however, and by asking for extra toast I managed to make up some very acceptable marmalade sandwiches which I smuggled out for later. John came to check up on me on the third day and told me not to worry about the lack of orders. "They will be back to order on the last two days." And sure enough they were. By the time the fair closed I had orders for three-quarters of all the cosies, and the tea-cosy business was up and running.

Back home to my surprise the family had managed quite well without me, although you would not have thought it from the list of complaints. David had run short of clean clothes, not being able to see the pile of clean washing sitting on top of his chest of drawers, and the two youngest were a bit miffed at having to negotiate with their eldest brother for lifts to various places in mother's car. I have no wish to make it appear easy for a woman to run a business, even from home, because it is not. Even when the pressures of my involvement with the practice lifted due to the building of a fully staffed medical centre, it only needed one of the boys to become ill, the car to fail, or my mother to throw a wobbly, and the carefully built pack of cards would fall. And there were quite a few occasions when I bit off more than I could chew and David would have to turn to and help me when he eventually got back from the surgery.

After all, when I married David in the mid 1950s a wife was expected to put her husband and family first in return for a roof and a meal ticket for life. Not only did my mother worry abut the time "my little things" were beginning to take up, but Dame Barbara Cartland took me to task as well. She maintains that women must make sure their menfolk are properly looked after when they come home from a hard day's work, and the wife must make an effort to look feminine and beautiful for her husband. As she said, "Poor David." I have always been grateful he did not make more fuss about my business ventures. How much was due to complete exhaustion on his part from the hours he worked, which could have caused him not to notice my absences as long as there was something to eat and wear I do not know, but looking back the escalation of the tea-cosy business and attendances at the trade fairs took up a fair amount of time, and I ended up working even longer hours than he did.

I have to say it was good fun, and the anticipation of how many orders one might get at each show made up for the pain and grief. Travelling to the fair venue and setting up the products was not easy on one's own, even with something light and easy to transport like the cosies. Frances managed to combine pregnancies and rearing babies with designing and producing an ever expanding range of cosies, but could not be expected to help at the shows or take much part in the selling in the early days.

Shortly after the success of the Torquay show the first International Trade Gift Fair was launched at the Birmingham Exhibition Centre. We booked a tiny space for an enormous amount of money, but when I got there I discovered we had been given a much bigger area than I expected. As I had travelled up to Birmingham by train with the entire Almond-Worters display in a suitcase this was not as good as it seemed, and I was nearly arrested after trying to change the venue of a potted palm of which there seemed to be an enormous number just lying idle. The Queen was due to visit and every leaf, much less plant, was accounted for. And no way was it possible to "acquire" anything like a table or chair for the stand. The rules and regulations started at the perimeter of the Exhibition Centre, and covered everything from deliveries, parking, hire of chairs, lights, and floor coverings; to change a light bulb oneself could bring out the entire electrical trade union members. There were hundreds of stands, the majority beautifully designed and set up with very expensive fittings, and manned by beautiful people. Depending on the location of one's stand it could be extremely hot or very cold and draughty, and although there were exhibitors' lounges and cafeterias, if you were manning your stand on your own as I was, these were out of bounds. It also paid to be near the lavatories or have a strong bladder. At first I was sure that if I left the stand for a moment that would be the precise second a buyer from America or Harrods would arrive.

Gradually I lost some of my trepidation, especially as the cosies proved to be ever more popular. Many of the buyers from the National Trust and stately homes that I already supplied with my own line of goods would come on the stand for a rest and a chat, and over the years became good friends. In particular I soon realised that some of the Lords and Dukes and their Ladies who came to look round felt quite threatened by the heavy sales patter of some of the more commercially orientated stands, especially if they were opening their homes for the first time. They were grateful not to be pressurised into having a large minimum order, although I got a fair amount of stick from Frances if I let them have an order for half-a-dozen assorted cosies.

The store buyers always remained a bit daunting. They invariably moved round the shows in small groups, both the men and the women power-dressed (how expressive that is), and all clutched extremely expensive brief cases. A frisson of excitement would precede them down the line of stands, but they would never appear to look especially at anything. It was only later that a minion would reappear with an order form already filled in to negotiate as much of a discount as possible. It was extremely important not to give so much of a discount in the excitement of taking a large order that it left us with hardly any profit at all. One of the unscrupulous ways of getting a low price was to put in a really big order to be delivered in two or three parts, then cancelling after the first delivery having taken advantage of the full discount.

The foreign buyers could also prove a problem,

especially if their English was not as good as they thought. For several years a group of Japanese used to arrive on the stand and I have to say I dreaded their visit even when charmed by their habit of all bowing and hissing gently at me, rather like Muscovy ducks. It was difficult to explain what a tea-cosy or coffee-cosy was. When we added egg-cosies, in different little English country cottage designs, I was quite taken aback to have them put in an order for several hundred, as we seemed to be on a totally different wavelength as to what they were for. After they had bowed themselves off the stand and gone hissing gently down the aisle the man from the next door stand said he was sure they had ordered them to go on golf clubs. Whatever they bought them for, we did not get a repeat order which was a shame. The run for 100 metres of printed cloth for egg-cosies produced 5,000, and although this was before the salmonella egg scare it was an awful lot of cosies. The designs were really colourful, a little brick house, a flint-faced cottage, a thatched cottage, a black-and-white timbered cottage, and a little Kentish half-timbered cottage. Sitting among a pile of them as I made up some scented sachets of my own, I realised they too would make little pot-pourri bags if sewn up along the bottom with a loop of velvet ribbon added at the top. With a bit of adaptation they also made up into neck purses, this time sewn up along the bottom and with a zip along the top, although it took me some time to trace a source of cord to hang them round the neck which conformed to the regulations governing the breaking strain of the neck cord in case anyone should strangle themselves!

You would not think that something as innocuous as a tea-cosy could generate such a mountain of regulations and paperwork to export, but they did. Great though it was to have orders from over 14 countries each one had its regulations, and it was the exporter's responsibility to get it right. I discovered the hard and expensive way that F.O.B. meant free on board, and after a tearful phone call from me Richard (Frances' husband) had to drive down to the docks with a large order for New York. In the end I tried to make sure all export orders could be posted, or if too big could be delivered to a central warehouse. Even posting presented problems. All boxes have to be less than a certain maximum size which is able to fit into a postman's regulation size sack, and the sack's neck must be able to be drawn tight. It can also become difficult if someone behind the post office counter is extra bolshie and the box will not go through the hatch. It was never advisable to try and get an order away on pension day, as any major hold up at the front of the queue incited the OAPs to bang their sticks and mutter. Now I am one myself of course, I see their point.

I will draw a veil over the customs forms, and the gradually mounting difficulties of guaranteeing payment from different parts of the world, preferably in sterling, without it costing us too much. After a particularly gruelling visit to the bank I happened to say that our leader (at that time Mrs Thatcher) was surely encouraging us to export or die, or words to that effect, to which the manager replied rather cuttingly he thought perhaps she was thinking more of cars and aeroplanes than tea-cosies.

Tea-, coffee- and egg-cosies they might only have been but we had begun to get quite a few special orders for a complete run of an individually designed cosy. The first one was the frontage of Jackson's of

Piccadilly, the specialist grocers, which has now unfortunately closed. It was a lovely design, with the shop windows overhung with red canopies, and little bay trees in the entrances. Packed in its plastic bag with a header giving the history of the shop it made a very smart and unusual present. More difficult was a request for Frances to design a tea-cosy for the Scilly Isles to encapsulate what the Scilly Isles represented, and all from a picture postcard. Frances did her best to try and dissuade the shop keeper who was only too keen to have 500 done. She was not happy with the design she produced of an archway through which was a glimpse of a fort, all behind a sea of daffodils, and I was not happy he would sell them all. A tea-cosy we produced for the Royal National Rose Society of their headquarters near St Albans was very different and looked very nice indeed, as did Beningborough Hall for the National Trust.

After the fruit and vegetable market was moved out of Covent Garden and the buildings were refurbished to make a pedestrian shopping centre, Frances designed a cosy for the Covent Garden General Store. This design was oblong with four sides, which led me to think of producing a toaster cover, and an appliance cover. The toaster cover was a bit dodgy having to have adequate warnings about making sure the toaster was turned off, unplugged and cool before covering it, and I was still a bit nervous about it. Dire thoughts of being sued if someone set fire to their kitchen haunted me. The appliance cover worked very well after we had settled on a size to fit the most popular appliances. It was a smart late 18th century house, built for the wealthy merchants of that era. Similar houses can be seen in London, now smart flats or embassies.

With Frances well into her third pregnancy and confined in more ways than one to Kent, partnership meetings invariably took place down there, and I fell in love with the oast-houses. I was always saying how nice they would look as a cosy, and Frances eventually said that if I could think of something to go under them she would design it, but no way would they make a tea-, coffee- or egg-cosy. Playing round with a bit of surplus quilting I made up a very rough design based on the shape of an oast house and then looked round for something to go underneath it. Eureka - a toilet roll. Rushing into the next room to show David, I was a bit taken aback when he said "Oh yes dear, very nice, but who would want warm toilet paper?"

In spite of David's fears, and the snide remarks from some of my friends, the toilet roll cover proved so popular that Frances had to produce another oast house design, and I think we must have ousted many a knitted poodle or crinoline lady from the lavatory shelf. I was quite surprised at the reaction from some people to the success of our business. Having tea with Dame Barbara and telling her how hurtful I found it she told me not to worry, she had the same problem! "It's just jealousy, darling. On the whole women friends do not like you to do well, and anyway, for some reason we British are embarrassed and even ashamed of success." I suppose I was inclined to take remarks too personally, particularly about the products I had slaved over to get just right, and then worked hard to find the right outlet.

Frances found it very difficult when she started to do the trade fairs if people stood and discussed her designs in front of her in uncomplimentary terms. She said it was as bad as somebody criticising her children. I know a lot of people hanker after being self-employed, but one has to be both physically and mentally very tough. If you stop for a cup of coffee you are not earning, if you are ill there is no sick pay, and if you make a mistake there is no-one else to blame. On the other hand all the rewards are yours if you get it right. I got a great kick out of sticking the Design Centre labels on quite a few of my products and the tea-cosy designs, and when items were chosen to appear in magazines. Being written up in the local paper was good fun too, and thinking back I probably did show off a bit! It was good to have something to talk about at dinner parties other than children, but as time passed and women were expected to have a career I felt sorry for the ones who were full time housewives and mothers, they seemed to feel they had to apologise when asked what they did. Dame Barbara tried to redress the balance by asking for mothers to receive a salary for staying at home as they do in Sweden, but nothing came of it.

1) Myself, Dame Barbara, David

2) David and Submarine Commander Captain Merten

3) A favourite teacosy

4) A youthful Elizabeth I

5) A cot is not enough

6) An Albanian with Kalashnikov is not to be messed with!

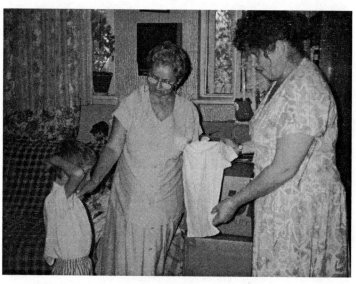

7) Dr. Matusa and Christine sizing up Marian for a new shirt

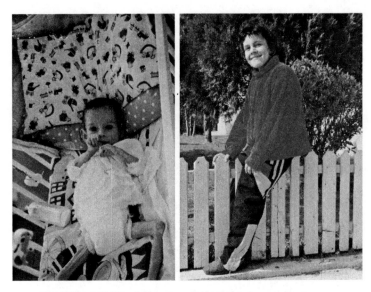

8) and 9) Daniella when I first saw her and now

10) At the Black sea with Alexandru

11) Skinny Petru, Alexandru, Aurelia, Toady, Marian, Costel – all have died

12) My own private army! Alexander, Harry, Florence, Miles, Dominic, Benjamin, Matthew

13) Katerina and friend

14) The House of Solomon

Chapter 8

A Leaf From the Pages of History
* * * * * * * * * *

With the tea-cosies doing well and Frances able to give more time to that business, I was able to concentrate on developing more of my own lines. I had reluctantly given up the pottery although I promised myself I would get back to it one day. It really was very labour intensive (mine), and was not something I could easily fit in between quiet moments in the rest of the business. I also found as time passed that heaving large lumps of cold wet clay did not do my back or my hands much good. What I could fit in was researching the history of a particular place to see if I could produce something relevant which would be of special interest to visitors. For St. Albans Abbey in Hertfordshire this was easy with such a long and interesting history.

In AD 303 a Roman soldier called Alban gave his life for a Christian priest and became our first Christian martyr. He was sentenced to death in the Roman basilica, parts of which are still visible behind the Roman Museum in St Michael's, and then he was marched to the top of the hill where the Abbey now stands to be beheaded. It is said that rose bushes along the way came into bloom as he passed to his death. The tradition remains to this day that a service is held every year on Rose Sunday in July. The congregation all bring a rose and the climax is a vast procession which winds its way from the nave past the high altar to the tomb of Alban where everyone throws their rose.

As a child, living near the Abbey as I did, I always loved that service, the tomb became a beautiful mound of every conceivable colour and shape of rose, and the smell was quite overpowering. I used to daydream in more boring services about how I was going to have a rose service held for me without going to such extremes as having my head cut off. In the meantime I had to make do with producing a packet of rose pot-pourri for the Abbey with a card giving the history, and the quotation I found in an old book. "So among the roses of the martyrs brightly shines St. Alban."

A small church was built on the spot where Alban was put to death and buried, and in the 8th century King Offa founded the Abbey there, together with a monastery and a splendid sepulchre for Alban's bones. In 1077 the first Norman abbot enlarged the Abbey, using bricks from the ruins of Roman Verulamium. The tower, which is still standing, is therefore made of bricks almost twice as old as itself. Unfortunately the monastery in particular did not escape the attentions of Henry VIII in the middle of the 16th century, and not much of it now remains. However, in its heyday the monks used to give the poor of St. Albans bowls of soup, and on Good Friday in 1361 a monk called Father Rocliff made some small spiced buns, and marked them with the sign of the cross for the poor to have with their soup. These proved so popular that the bun custom for Good Friday spread, but it was said that nowhere were they as good as those made at St Albans. The custom died out with the destruction of the monastery, but in 1850 a baker called Collier launched the buns in London, claiming they were from Father Rocliff's original recipe. He sold many hundreds that first Good Friday at eight for six old pennies, and the tradition of hot cross buns as we know it was established.

I put all this on a card, together with a recipe for the buns, and added a wooden spoon tied with ribbons of the blue and yellow colours of St. Albans. Adding a packet of the spices needed it made a very good memento for the Abbey to sell in their shop. I admit to one or two false starts before I perfected this, mostly to do with the recipe. The first buns I made, sticking as closely as I could to the original recipe from the Old Boke of St. Alban, were according to David and the boys more like medieval cannon balls. The second batch, with modifications, were all right eaten hot, but had a shelf life of 30 minutes before they again hardened.

It was with great difficulty that I tore myself away from all the interesting books on the history of St. Albans, and particularly the area round the Abbey. Right next to it is a piece of land called the Martyrs' plot, where Richard II watched the death of 15 peasants involved with Wat Tyler in the ill fated Peasants Revolt of 1350. Next to that is the only part of the Monastery still standing, the great gateway, which is now part of St. Albans School. This school was founded in 946, and built up a fine reputation till it was shut by Henry VIII. Luckily Elizabeth I ordered it to be reopened, and all my three boys attended it. My middle son showed true entrepreneurial spirit by hiring himself out during the lunch hour to be photographed outside the school gates to passing tourists, giving them the benefit of his mother's researches into the history of the surrounding area and charging them the equivalent of 15p a time. Unfortunately the school authorities did not view this in the same spirit as his mother.

Another place of special interest is Salisbury Hall near London Colney, now no longer open. Within easy reach of London by fast coach and horses, (necessary when royalty could not trust Parliament), Charles II found this the ideal weekend retreat for himself and his mistress Nell Gwynne. I was asked whether I would like to run a shop during the summer when the house was open to the public. Who could resist the challenge? It was only to be open on Thursday and Sunday afternoons and the shop was to be in Nell Gwynne's cottage. This was on the edge of the moat and where Nell Gwynne, in desperation at not getting recognition for one of her bastard children by the king, held the baby out of the window over the water and threatened to drop him in. Eventually the King shouted "Save the Duke of St Albans!" and Nell retrieved the baby. Unfortunately, in spite of the fact that there was, and still is, an aircraft museum by the side of the hall, containing among other things the wooden prototype of the de Havilland Mosquito, not many tourists seemed to be aware of Salisbury Hall. Although not a financial success or popular with my family who expected not only the usual large Sunday lunch, but the serving wench to go with it and to clear up afterwards, I did have time to wander about the grounds.

There was a beautiful lime tree with the remains of a tree house in it, said to be where Winston Churchill used to retire for peace and quiet to write some of his more fiery speeches. It was also said that nothing would grow beneath the tree because Churchill used to crumple up and throw out pieces he had written and was not pleased with and they were so fiery they scorched the earth. A nice tale, but of course nothing grows under a lime tree of that size as the branches almost touch the ground and are so leafy they shut out the light. I suppose because trees have such a long life there are many legends and tales told about them. At Hatfield House there used to be the old oak tree that Princess Elizabeth was said to have been sitting under when the message came that Mary had died, and she was now Queen Elizabeth I. While delivering to Stratfield Saye, the home of the Dukes of Wellington, I had noticed a splendid turkey oak, which was apparently planted by the first Duke of Wellington on the grave of Copenhagen, the charger which carried him into the battle of Waterloo.

All these trees, the lime, the oak and the turkey oak, have very distinctive leaves, and I remembered seeing some very nice real leaves, plated in 22 carat gold, made into pendants and brooches. Why not these leaves, boxed up with a card giving the history of the tree? It took quite some time to track down a company who did this sort of thing, and was prepared to plate leaves I sent them. It was quite a process, involving plating the leaves firstly in copper, then silver and then gold. The leaves had to be freshly picked, not too young, and carefully packed, otherwise they would rot or curl up and dry out before they were plated. Then I had to convince the stately home owner it was a good idea, as the jewellery was of course quite expensive by the time it was on the shelves. Blenheim Palace had just lost its avenue of beautiful elms, but they had wonderful copses of beech, planted by Capability Brown, and these made elegant pendants and brooches. Even the Royal National Rose Society had their leaves plated, although my hands got well and truly pricked by the thorns, trying to get evenly sized leaves without any blemishes.   Caterpillar doo-doos were the bane of my life.

I was still disappointed about not being able to do an Elizabethan Oak at Hatfield House, the original tree died of old age a short time before I contacted them. My first suggestion, to shift the notice about Elizabeth to the next oak in line which was younger and healthier, was dismissed out of hand.   My second suggestion, that one of the other very old broad oaks must have been sat under by Cromwell while studying his map to see where London was, was also thrown out.   When I repeated this last suggestion during a talk on local history to a WI meeting, I received a very short sharp letter from the then curator of Hatfield House who said this was how fables started.   I thought it was quite a nice fable myself but there you are.

At Camfield Place shortly after, having tea with Dame Barbara, I was bemoaning the lack of an Elizabeth I oak when she told me that I need not worry. In the grounds of Camfield Place grew a great old oak which was planted by Elizabeth when she was a Princess and being kept prisoner at Hatfield Palace. Hatfield House had not been built at that time.   She used to be allowed to hunt in the surrounding countryside and killed her first stag in Squire Camfield's grounds.   She not only planted an oak on the spot, but returned quite a few times to hunt and dine with Squire Camfield with her retinue, and nearly bankrupted him.   Dame Barbara was delighted with the result of gold plating not only the leaves from this tree but some acorns as well, and many and famous are the people who now own "A leaf (or acorn) from the pages of history".

This particular tree was to lead me into trouble.

After a few years Dame Barbara began to ask me why the leaves and acorns appeared to be lucky for people. She had them ringing her up, after they had been given one, and telling her their luck had changed since wearing her gift. On one occasion in particular a famous astrologer had insisted that someone he met wearing a leaf had an aura of luck surrounding them and had rung her to know why. Jokingly, I said perhaps it was because I was supposed to be a white witch. When I was small, my grandmother used to take me to visit an old friend of hers. In those days a child was definitely seen and not heard, but I was quite content to sit in the window and play with a box of buttons of all shapes and sizes. The other thing that fascinated me, and I spent a lot of time staring at it, was a glass witch's ball hanging in the window. As it turned in any slight breeze the sun caught it, and the colours turned from green to blue. If you stared at it long enough shadows turned into faces and figures. Before the old lady died she gave it to my grandmother to keep for me. She had always been acknowledged as a white witch but she had no children to hand her magic power on to, but was convinced it should come to me. When my grandmother died she had left a letter to say I was to have the ball and what her old friend had said.

My mother let me hang it in our sitting room window, and I was quite taken aback when over the years one or two people would look at it and ask who owned the witch's ball. Later on I tried to find out a bit more about the significance of it, but could only find that these glass balls were hung up to keep away the evil or black witches. White witches were usually "old crones", who had knowledge of simples and herbs used for healing and the good of people, although in times gone-by they had to be very careful not to be mistaken for the evil kind, and find themselves thrown into a pond to drown for their trouble.

When I married, the ball came with me, and not having a suitable window I tied it to the central light fitting, knotting the chain it hung from several times. The day after I jokingly said I was a white witch I came downstairs to find the chain had somehow untied itself and the ball had fallen on the floor, smashed into a thousand pieces! At that moment the telephone rang and a friend told me to switch on the radio as Dame Barbara Cartland was talking to Tony Blackburn about my lucky leaves and that I was a white witch. This was taken up by a magazine and I began to receive requests from strangers for a lucky leaf to change their luck, together with a litany of bad luck from which they had been suffering. One lady even wanted a lucky leaf to be able to have a baby. I was horrified, but David just laughed and said it served me right.

I rang my famous friend to ask her what on earth I should do, and she told me not to be so feeble, but to send any letters like that down to her and her secretaries would deal with them. Luckily it was all a nine-days' wonder, but when I remember it a small shiver runs down my back. I had no idea how superstitious people could be, or how superstitious I was.

The other line of jewellery I was developing gave me trouble of a different sort. This jewellery was made from polished pudding stone, said to be over 60 million years old, and considered by geologists to be rarer than gold. It is also supposed to be unique to a small area of Hertfordshire. I believed it all until some know-it-all told me that a) it could be found elsewhere, b) there were tons of it, and c) most rocks are over 60 million years old. Too late, I had already printed the cards and started to market polished slabs of it (which I must say looked just like slices of plum pudding,) and smaller pieces let into silver and made into pendants.

No one else ever queried the date or the rarity, but further research on my part threw up the unpalatable fact that these lumps of pudding stone were considered magical, and were referred to as "breeding" or "growing" stones, as they tended to work their way up to the surface of the soil. Evidence existed of them being used for all sorts of purposes. The Romans used lumps of pudding stone as distance markers, and recent excavations near Hemel Hempstead showed that the Ancient Britons collected pudding stones to be used in burial mounds. The bit I particularly did not like was that lumps were placed on top of a coffin to make sure witches remained well and truly buried.

I had to go to a lapidary company to have the pudding stone polished. This was at a time when small craft tumblers were being made and marketed for people to polish their own stones, but pudding stone was such a hard conglomerate that only a commercial one would do the job. Unfortunately after a very short time even the commercial tumbler could not cope, but luckily I managed to get enough pieces done to run the line for two or three years. As a memento I had a large piece made into a pendant by a friendly silversmith, and I was particularly sorry to lose it in a burglary some time later.

Another product which was not too successful was Elizabethan perfumed ink. I had a great time researching this particular item. The history of ink starts from when primitive man dipped his finger in animal blood or the juice of plants and first made marks, but it was a long time before the first traces of ink as we know it today were found.

Some historians put the use of Indian ink as early as 2697 BC, but I discovered that for centuries people laboured hard to produce an indelible and easy-flowing liquid, and they used both simple and extremely complex methods, as well as ordinary and extraordinary ingredients. This could be a simple mixture of soot and water, or cuttle fish glands, or isinglass of donkey skin. Eventually the forerunner of our modern ink was discovered which consisted of fermented gall nuts which form on oak trees.

The Elizabethan housewife had to be able to make ink, and recipes were handed down and as jealously guarded as those for a special cake. In fact I found that ink recipes were quite often included in cookery books almost to the present day. Not since the Roman times had perfume been more lavishly used than during the Elizabethan era, and from the distillations of aromatic herbs and fragrant flowers in her stillroom the housewife, as a pretty conceit, used to add a few drops of perfume to her ink.

A pretty idea indeed. I cut a few corners by buying ink from a wholesaler, some little bottles from the local chemist, and added drops of essential oils from my herbal supplier. Unfortunately the bottles leaked and to get the ink to smell of anything except ink I had to add far too much oil. This was not only very expensive but changed the consistency. At the same time I had set my heart on producing some quill pens, but this idea was soon to prove unworkable. The best quill pens were made from the pinion feathers of goose, or at a pinch, turkey. There seemed to be very few geese about, and these were definitely in need of their own pinion feathers, certainly until Christmas. The modern turkey is bred to mature, as far as its flesh is concerned, at a young age, but its feathers remain too immature to make a nice sturdy pen. I was not prepared to compromise and insert a biro into a quill, and reluctantly gave up the idea.

I think I could have gone on for ever researching and producing new ideas, but the years were flying past. The boys had finished university and gone on to acquire jobs, homes and then wives. I admit I had put some heavy pressure on them to hurry up and make me a legitimate grandma before I was too old, so I have only myself to blame for what happened next. When the grandchildren started to arrive the boys expected I should at least be about to get the full benefit. They also pointed out that poor old Dad was getting near retirement age, and as I had always said I was only working to fill in time until he was at home more, perhaps now was the time to start slowing down and being at home myself.

Reluctantly I withdrew from the tea-cosy business, but found the other products just filled up any spare time I might have had. Over the next year or so I found people to take on the various lines until by Christmas 1988 the last box, sack, and bale of raw materials had been handed on. And then what was I to do?

Chapter 9

Kalashnikovs and Kisses
* * * * * * * * *

For most of the next year I tried to catch up with what I felt I had missed while I was working such long hours. I joined every club in sight, went to all the local coffee mornings (as an onlooker this time), ruined my neck and made the local osteopath despair by trying to start up my pottery again, took up spinning and weaving, tried my hand at painting, and even cleaned the house and sorted the garden. David showed no signs of taking any earlier retirement than his allotted span, and with only one grandson so far by the Christmas of 1989 I was so bored I was watching a lot of television.

And that is where I was, sitting in front of the television, when those horrendous pictures were shown on the Anneka Rice programme, "Challenge Anneka", of the children in the orphanages in Romania. Those rusting cots, jammed together like battery hen cages, filled with what looked like Belsen babies, haunted me day and night. Having just become a proud grandparent, every time I looked at my own plump grandson I saw in my mind's eye those other babies. So it was a relief when I saw in the local paper that a collection was being made of soap powder, toilet paper and household goods to go on a convoy of lorries to Romania, under the leadership of a vicar and his parish from over the border in Essex. That was something I could help with.

Luckily I still had my small van so I rang round a few people asking for some soap or a few packets of soap powder, which I could pick up and then take down to the collection point when I had a van full. All was going well and then I had a call from a friend's husband who had heard I was collecting soap powder. Did I want three tons going spare and if so where would I like it delivered? It was the first of many similar calls, and alerted me to what a really wasteful society we are. Should there be a misprint in the printing of the labels, or perhaps a corner of a pallet of tins get knocked, it is cheaper to dump the stuff than repack or relabel. Wrong orders, unwanted late deliveries, over-runs on the production line, it apparently makes economic sense to destroy the goods. If they can be transported to places where they are going to be used and there is no likelihood of them being sold then that is another matter, but someone has to stand the cost of the transportation. I had opened a Pandora's box of goodies, but as neither the Essex convoy nor the collection centre could cope unless a lorry could be found and paid for I nearly gave up there and then. But those little children haunted me, and when I discovered a lorry would cost £2,000 and it was roughly 2,000 miles there and back to the delivery point in Romania I felt someone was trying to tell me something, apart from my friends that is, who were telling me I was mad! I put out an appeal for help to get the stuff out by asking for £1 a mile. To my surprise money started flowing in. I think that programme on television had touched a lot of people's hearts, and an opportunity to help with something as direct as this, appealed to them.

By the time the vicar came back from that first journey I had raised almost the whole amount. When I phoned him to tell him he took the wind out of my sails by saying what he had seen out there had changed his mind completely as to what sort of help these children needed. From the television and newspaper reports most of us thought that the children were orphans, kept in terrible conditions, and dying through neglect and lack of basic facilities and care. In fact most of the children had parents but were part of President Ceaucescu's fearful legacy to Romania.

During the years before he was overthrown he had decided to increase the population to help achieve his dreams of wealth and power. He wanted to change Romania from a mainly agricultural country to an industrial one, and for that he needed manpower. Women were told they had to have at least five children. It is easy for us to say we would never, in this country, submit to such a demand. But if you live in a police state, where your every-day needs are only met if you obey, and you can be fined or be turned onto the streets if you do not, it can change things. I was also told later by some of the Romanian women that they were subjected to frequent examinations with a policeman present, and if they could not give an adequate reason for not being pregnant they could be put in prison. To gain control over his people Ceaucescu had already had many of the smallholdings and houses bulldozed flat, and the peasant farmers and their families moved into tall blocks of badly-built flats where they became dependent on the State for their food and fuel. With the subsequent shortage of food, no adequate antenatal care and no money to be wasted on extra training for nurses (he considered women should know by instinct how to nurse), births were not registered for six months to hide the dreadfully high mortality rate both from the outside world and the Romanian people.

Women had to have all their babies in hospitals, and those born underweight, with disabilities, or failing to thrive, were put into institutions. Once in the system it was very difficult to get them out again and most mothers gave up the struggle. Quite a few babies were left behind in the hospitals by mothers who could not cope with any more children and swelled the numbers in these institutions or "orphanages". Once there, through totally inadequate provision for their care, they continued to fail to thrive, and then they began to die.

In the town of Constanta, the main port for Romania on the Black Sea, a Doctor Matusa, in charge of the infectious diseases department of the hospital there, could not understand why so many of these children and others in her care were dying from childhood diseases from which they should have recovered in far greater numbers, even though some of them were not receiving an adequate diet. They were also beginning to die of diseases, particularly certain types of cancer, seen only in adults. Living and working in a seaport she was occasionally able to get hold of medical journals from abroad, and in one of these journals read an article written by a professor from Newark, New Jersey, in which he described his work among children suffering from HIV and AIDS. To her horror she began to believe this might be what these children were dying of, and after she got hold of some testing kits her fears proved correct.

To this day no-one can say quite how it all started. It was unfortunate as David told me that Romania is one of those countries where people believe more in the curative power of an injection than in pills or medicines. One theory is that Madame Ceaucescu, when she heard the new work force in the institutions was not thriving, ordered minute injections of blood as a tonic and cheap alternative to providing vitamin pills or extra food. Blood was not donated in Romania, it was bought; many of the prostitutes in Constanta sold their blood as a regular thing, and because it was a seaport HIV could have spread this way. Needles were re-used without adequate sterilisation in schools in the vaccination programmes, and blood given in transfusions in hospitals was not tested for HIV. Whatever the cause, it is now known that out of the people HIV positive in the UK only one or two per cent are children, compared with 85 per cent in Romania.

When Dr Matusa began to realise not only the problem but the size of it, she reported her findings to the Government authorities, but Ceaucescu refused to recognise that Romania had AIDS. In the meantime children continued to sicken and die in the overcrowded institutions, and word began to spread of a dreadful infectious disease, which once caught, killed you. Is it any wonder that the untrained women left in charge, inadequately paid and ill-equipped to deal with such a disease, handled the sick children as little as possible and had to leave them in their cots in the sort of conditions we saw them in on television? David wonders how, even in this country, with all the social services at our beck and call, we would have managed with so many affected children; and after all we have constant hot water, disposable nappies and plenty of soap powder. Unfortunately one of the unpleasant side effects of HIV is diarrhoea, and in some institutions the helpers only had bits of cardboard to scrape it off the children's bottoms, cold water a couple of hours a day, and only minute amounts of soap allocated per month.

I do not know what the outcome would have been had Ceaucescu and his regime not been overthrown at that point, allowing Dr Matusa to start her work in earnest and the rest of the world to become aware of the terrible plight of these children.

So when the vicar came back from Romania having found out the true situation with the children, he decided the only thing to do was to build a hospice for them to come in to die in clean conditions and with loving care. A site was found in a town on the banks of the Danube within reach of Constanta; a charity was set up under the directorship of the vicar, and having managed to raise enough money to send out the lorry loaded with goods, I hastily changed the appeal to "Buy a Brick for £1". And that was the end of my "retirement".

David came out with me to Romania and was as devastated as I was at the state of the children. He gave me tremendous support and encouragement over the next few years and during that time I managed to raise nearly a quarter of a million pounds for the charity. As word spread, other people were fund-raising as hard up and down the country, and within a year of standing on a muddy site in Romania and wondering how on earth anything would ever be built on it, David and I were back out helping to make a four-storey custom-built hospice ready to receive the first children. None of us who were lucky enough to be there at that time will ever forget it. The hospice was still in a sea of mud, overlaid with snow and ice, the temperature was in the minus 2Os, the house in the grounds for the British carers and nurses was only meant for about 15 and had double that number, the heating had gone off and the pipes in the house had burst. Live wires dangled from the ceilings in the hospice, cables snaked up through the front door, the place was swarming with workmen and no-one could make the cook understand that we would need soup and warm milk when the children arrived.

Dr Matusa had been appointed the Medical Director of the hospice and was responsible, together with representatives from the Romanian Government and the local institutions, for sending the children most in need of care to the hospice, in accordance with the conditions laid down by the charity that it should be for children with around three months left to live. Because there were so many children known to be terminally ill, and only the one hospice in the whole of Romania for them, it was felt this was the best way to make sure as many as possible could come in for the short time left to them to know some tender loving care. Little did any of us guess we would be faced with another problem, one which we were all thrilled about but had made no provision for.

Also unknown to us, there had been a certain amount of fear and prejudice in the town about having a place where children dying of the dreaded disease AIDS were going to be brought. To start with it was difficult to get local help, and women prepared to come in to be trained in the care of these terminally ill children. After the first children were in I noticed people crossing the road to the other side when walking past the hospice, and covering up their children's faces with scarves. Within a few months all that had changed, and as there is no word in Romanian for hospice, it was known as The House of Love.

David says that in Britain the hospice would never have been allowed to even contemplate taking in children in the state it was in that day in February 1992.

The British volunteers had worked 18 hours a day, doctors, nurses and helpers, scrubbing out wards and storerooms, sifting through tons of goods and carrying them down to the basement or up three flights of stairs to the various wards. Flat packs had to be opened and the cots assembled, mattresses retrieved from under ceiling-high piles of equipment, sheets found, mobiles hung up and supplies of nappies stored ready. The night before the first eight children were due we stood on the ward looking at the empty cots with their matching duvets and a little bedside locker for each one, cuddly toys in place. The whole ward was spotless and bright with coloured friezes and pictures, and we wondered what the next day and the days ahead would bring. Not a few of us, even the trained ones, wondered whether we could cope and rise to the challenge. When we were up to the full complement of children, it would still be the largest children's hospice in the world, even though the original estimate of 100 cots had to be revised. This number was found to be impossible to achieve if we were to maintain the quality of care.

On our previous visit to Romania David and I had been to the hospital in Constanta, to the local hospital, and to two or three "orphanages", and although I thought I knew what to expect, nothing, but nothing, could prepare one for the sight of these children. Only sufficient money was allocated to provide one carer to 30 children in some of the establishments. To be able to get round them all, feed, clean and change them meant that bottles had to be left propped up in the cots; as the children got weaker and more ill they were unable to manage to feed themselves properly, and together with their chronic diarrhoea became emaciated and helpless. Wards full of what looked like babies, with huge eyes and stick-like arms and legs, lying in total silence or as one journalist put it, making a noise grinding their teeth which sounded like the wind rustling through dry grass. And everywhere the smell. It was said that in some orphanages there was no money or provision for night staff, and the day staff locked the place up at eight at night, and went back at six the next morning. Children who died would be labelled, and if no-one claimed the body it would be sent down to the municipal dump. One child who came to the hospice had lost fingers and part of an ear. It was said that she had been thought dead and left at a dump which was over-run with rats.

It was not just the unwanted and dying children who had nothing. Conditions were as bad for most of the people in the town. The local hospital was in one of the badly built blocks of flats, designed to house families in one- or two-bedroomed apartments. The maternity ward had four beds crammed into each tiny room, the mothers gave birth on a bloodstained table in another small room, and then the babies were placed, often two or three to a cot, in another room. The mothers were allowed to go and see their babies to feed them only every four hours. If they were unable to feed them, old Coca-Cola bottles seemed to be used with bits of rag as teats. There were only four lavatories for the whole hospital, and when we saw them two had overflowed onto the floor. When David asked the doctor what he needed he said he could do with some bandages; when we asked him about dressings he said he had never had any of those. David had to return home to England, and I have a feeling that a few of his regular "whingers" at the surgery got quite short shrift from him!

It was not surprising, when aid started to arrive at the institutions, that it was pilfered before reaching the children. After what I saw out there I really could not put my hand on my heart and say I would not steal for my grandchildren if I were in a similar position. After the usual bad press about things going missing and the aid not reaching where it should, not only was it increasingly difficult to get people at home to donate, but the people in charge of the institutions locked away the toys and clothes so that when visitors from Britain and other countries called they could be shown the goods were being kept safely in the cupboards and had not been stolen - much less played with or worn. In the end I personally felt the only solution was to send so much stuff out that there would be more than enough both for the locals and the children. Things, of course, have come a long way and conditions are very different today, thank goodness.

That first moment in 1992 when the ambulance, donated from my own home town, arrived in the grounds, and the first little bundles were carried into the hospice, was nothing less than a miracle, made possible by the generosity of so many people. As each bundle of blankets was unwrapped, and the children were carefully laid into their brand new Mothercare cots, there was hardly a dry eye in the house. This after a short time included the children! At the start we were unable to communicate with them or they with us. We had very little in the way of medical notes and no indication whether they could manage a spoon or should have a bottle. Overcome by the sheer colour of the ward and the noise and movement round them, some cried, some tried to hide under their blanket, and some were quite rigid with fear.

Mealtime brought wails, screams and tears, and a lot of food ended up on the floor. The chef had been asked to provide soup, and had certainly done his best, but it was minestrone Romanian-style, which with all the shortages at that time meant the meat was mostly fat and gristle. Most of the children did not seem able to cope with anything in their mouths that needed chewing as they had only ever had gruel. In the end we decided to try and put it into bottles, but minestrone is not built for baby bottles and with the subzero temperatures outside the ward and up the two flights of stairs from the kitchen the fat congealed as it hit the glass. Eventually it was decided to abandon the soup and make up some milk, but the only two unbroken jugs had "vanished" and there was nothing bigger than a coffee mug to make it up in. Luckily I remembered unpacking a flower vase which at the time I had thought a daft thing to send out, but which was pressed into service. Cuddled up in loving arms, the children took every drop. Then once they were wiped, changed and tucked up in their beds, peace reigned.

During the next week two more wards were opened, pipes burst, power failed, workmen hammered and sawed, chaos reigned, but the children came in and before I left it was like watching thirsty flowers reviving in water. And slowly the heart of the "House of Love" began to beat. Rotas were organised, the chef stopped waving a large knife and shouting whenever he was told his cooking was not suitable for the children, the workmen started to spend more time on the wards talking and playing with the children, and acting as interpreters, and a routine for the children was established. Some of them were already beginning to emerge as little individuals, one in particular called George became the terror of Ward 1 very quickly. He had a stiff leg and was unable to talk, but could climb over the top of his cot and start dismantling his matching bedside cupboard in ten seconds flat by the second day, then finding this a bit boring managed to dismantle his neighbour's cot almost as fast. And as for the pretty mobiles. . . . . However, the day before I left he was poorly, and had retreated to his cot and put his head under his blanket and slept a lot, and we missed him. Nicko in Ward 2 was very different - he cried if handled and tried to bite. He was terrified to leave his cot and in the end the only way to lessen his distress was to lift him out straight into a cardboard box.

Reluctantly, I too had to return home, the fund-raising had to continue, inflation was beginning in Romania, most goods necessary for the comfort of staff and children were still unobtainable and had to be sent out by lorry.

*   *   *

I found I had to be careful to avoid both supermarkets and friends for a few days after I got back. Supermarkets with all their thousands of unnecessary goods, and overloaded trolleys made me feel quite sick. I was getting quite cross with friends asking me perfectly normal and well-meaning questions about what it was like "out there". Are the children really as poorly as they had been told, and do the things they donate really get there? It was even worse when I heard that the children I had begun to know and love were starting to die. I would wake up in the night crying, or tears would start running down my face driving along in the car. Worst of all was having to give the fund-raising talks to clubs and churches and show audiences photos of the children. It was my fault, but no-one had warned me not to become too involved. Anyway I defy anyone not to; even the professionals among us had trouble, and I am after all untrained in anything except being a grandmother.

By the time I got back to the hospice for a second visit it was summer and things had changed a lot. For a start there were no icicles growing out of the wall above my bed; in fact the temperature was up in the 90s. Some things had not changed: the pipes were not bursting but there was a water shortage, the food was erratic as ever and the chef had an even bigger knife to make his point.

The biggest change was on the wards. With dread in my heart as to how near death some of children must be - after all they were only expected to live three months when they first came in - I went straight up to see them. I was greeted by a wall of shouts, laughter, squeals of joy, all the children out of their cots and playing with toys. Even the most disabled were propped up or lay on blankets on the floor. And how they had *grown*. I was set upon by the more able-bodied and frisked for sweets, one of the first words they learnt. When I asked the nurse manager about the damage to their teeth of apparently unlimited sweets, she very gently pointed out that it really did not matter as they were not going to live that long. As I looked at them, it was so hard to remember they were all doomed to die.

As I write there is still no cure for AIDS. I wish some of our young people would listen to the warnings and not think it could not possibly happen to them. Death from AIDS, as I was to see, is not a pleasant one. The children seem to revive when they come into the hospice, and the problem I mentioned earlier is that instead of dying within a few months as expected, some of them are still alive and going strong after eight years. At the moment there is still no hope for them, but there has had to be a rethink on the length of their stay in the hospice. In fact a small school has had to be started as some of the children reached school age. Most of the children take to the school like ducks to water, and go off either to a room in the hospice or across the yard to the old nurses' home which has now been turned into a boarding school for the fitter children from the local orphanage.

However, wee Toady, so-called I am afraid to say because of his marked resemblance to a toad due to enlarged glands in his neck, and a very swollen stomach from an enlarged liver and spleen, did not take to school at all. He enquired whether there was going to be school in Heaven, and when told there need not be if he didn't want it, said he would go there then. After a further think he wanted to know what the food was like in Heaven, and decided on reflection he might as well stay where he was as he was quite happy with the food provided in the hospice.

This business of dying was one which had to be tackled with the children. They were mostly extremely bright, and soon knew that when a friend in the next cot became too ill to play they were probably going to die. In their short life they had become used to death, and luckily under the firm sure faith of the first lovely Irish nurse manager from Sligo, Sheila Donaghy, the children were given the confidence to face death without fear, and the nurses, helpers and carers to come to terms with it. Not that, as I have said, it was easy for any of us.

One of the first children to come in was a little boy I had seen in Constanta Hospital. Out of them all it was his face that stuck in my mind, even though he did not look among the illest. In Dr Matusa's hospital he had as much care as possible, but he was sitting in the corner of his cot, his hair dark and streaked with sweat and snot, and his face absolutely expressionless. He had TB, and an untreatable hernia because of his AIDS, his teeth were rotting in his head and he suffered from recurring ear infections. But he had such an adult look of hopelessness on his face. No child should look like that. So I was very pleased he had come to the hospice and managed to arrange to bath him and play with him when I could. Before I left he had developed a shy smile and could use a toy telephone, but his favourite word, in fact his only word, was "machina", Romanian for car. When I went out next I took a car magazine for him and some toy cars.

It is almost impossible not to have some children among them all who grow to mean more to you than others. Luckily every child without exception seems to become special to someone among the staff, and even with the pain it brings none of them begrudges it. Such a one was Alexandru (my eldest grandson's name is Alexander); he had fair hair when it was washed, (just like my grandson's) and his birthday was the same day as my middle grandson. He had developed meningitis when he was 18 months old, had been taken by his mother to Constanta hospital and been given a blood transfusion to save his life. Unfortunately the blood was contaminated and within a year he had developed AIDS, with all its attendant miseries. His mother, with two other small children, found it too difficult to cope and had left him in the hospital.

No-one minded me giving him a bit of extra attention. I felt he was sometimes overlooked because he was so quiet and amenable, but I could have been biased! There was a brief visit in the winter when I had to go out and help, three hectic days and nights trying to straighten out the stores and feeding the three men who had gone out to tackle the heating and ever bursting pipes in the nurses home, making life for the carers a misery after a heavy 12-hour shift on the wards. This time "my boy" was talking much more, smiling much more and could become quite as stroppy as my own grandchildren if things did not go his way. His eyes would light up when I came on the ward, but his eyebrows could come down and his lower lip come out and then watch out - I was delighted! Anything was better than that stony face. He was finding it difficult to keep his beloved machinas from the inquisitive fingers of other children on the ward, so along with the presents for the other children I sent him a bag to put them in, which was a great success, except that he insisted on dragging it everywhere, even into the bathroom, and fell asleep with it under him.

By the late summer of 1993, the hospice had been open for 18 months and was well settled in. More Romanian women were coming forward to work on the wards and learn to care for terminally ill children. Local children were coming in to visit, mothers were finding where their children had been taken and were beginning not only to visit but to ask to take them home for weekends if they were well enough. So far only a few children, all very frail when they arrived, had died, but even though the rest for the most part looked well, they tired easily and had a variety of diseases. This did not stop a party of soldiers from the band of the 16th/5th

Queen's Royal Lancers under the leadership of Bandmaster Graham Jones deciding to drive a bus, packed with disposable nappies and treats for the children and staff, all the way from England to the hospice and then taking them to the Black Sea for a day out. I must admit I was a bit worried about taking a busload of such sick children to the beach, but nothing would stop the lads and they planned it like a military operation. Nappies, potties, pushchairs, wet wipes, plasters, picnic, drinks, buckets, spades for the use of, it all went on board, and allocating each child to a carer or soldier, off we all went. And guess who I was just lucky enough to have as my charge for the day?

What a day we had - the soldiers sang to them and with them all the way down, keeping them supplied with endless sticky toffee and sweets on the two-hour journey. They had already been down and found the area of the beach suitable for the children, even though it meant parking in the car-park of a rather posh hotel. The children needed shade as their skin is extra sensitive to sun. I was rather anxious that the rest of the people on the beach would be worried at sharing it with children with AIDS, or the dreaded SIDA as it is called, but when they asked the Romanian helpers about the children and heard where they had come from we were inundated with gifts of ice-cream and the inevitable sweets. The manager of the hotel, coming out to see what the commotion was about, instead of turning us out of his car-park came out twice during the day with trays of cold drinks.

Some of the children just wanted to sit and look, some played in the sand, and some, like Alexandru, went for a paddle. It took them some time to summon up courage to put their feet in - after all for most of them it was their first sight of the sea. Then came the picnic, and after that a sleep, and not only for the children. The sight of a very large burly soldier fast asleep on his back in the sand with a very small child fast asleep on his chest like a barnacle on a rock will stay with me for ever. Back down to the sea, and this time Alex was straight in, up to his armpits and me up to my waist, followed by half a dozen of the others. I don't know who had more fun. Another round of unsuitable food, topped up by donations of salami and bread from the party next door, and back with everything onto the bus. To my surprise, no-one was sick, in fact everyone went to sleep again and the children did not even stir when we got back to the hospice and they were lifted out into their cots.

Many of those children have since died, some easily, some painfully slowly including my own Alexandru, but I hang on to that day when they all had so much fun and, just for a short time, discovered the joy of living.

The soldiers' visit was magic. The children responded to being looked after by men in contrast to the predominately female staff. They were not long back from the Gulf war, but like some of the macho lorry drivers on their first sight of the children, some shed unashamed tears. Then they rolled up their sleeves and waded in, sometimes quite literally at bath-time as the children after their initial fear of water managed to get more outside the bath than inside. They were growing heavier and bigger, and I for one found it a struggle to haul them in and out. The soldiers did not even flinch from nappy duty; again, with the children growing so large and the threat of hepatitis, disposable nappies were the only solution, but with the ever-present diarrhoea it was not a pleasant task.

Apart from all the much-needed supplies they had brought with them the soldiers had found room in their bus for their instruments, and also for the principal percussionist of the London Philharmonic Orchestra, Kevin Hatherway. The objective was to introduce the children to the therapy of music and rhythm. Romania has a long history of music and the lads thought that just because the children were not going to live very long it was no reason for them not to hear and learn a bit about music. Again, I thought they were expecting rather too much. Oh ye of little faith! When Kevin got at them with his marvellous array of instruments even the brain damaged ones responded. How they all enjoyed the music sessions! Most of us would have been thrilled to get the children just to bang on a drum, or shake a tambourine, but not Kevin, Graham and the band. Right from the word go the children had to do it right, with the right rhythm, and so they did.

Down in the town the orphanage brought out its children for a music session, and to see Kevin in action was magic. The children were eager to learn what to me seemed complicated rhythms on the instruments he had brought with him. They listened, they learnt, and they performed, and each session finished with a tremendous crocodile of dancing children, all singing and playing, following Kevin and his drum like the Pied Piper. He even managed to sweep up the rather stern-faced staff of the orphanage who samba-ed with the best of them. Wherever there were people, and in particular children, the band and Kevin played. In the town square, in the old people's homes, in an asylum, in the hospitals, and even in the sea at Constanta! And everywhere the people and children responded to the rhythms.

In the hospice was a girl called Gabriella, known as Gaby.   She was seven years old, mentally and physically handicapped, HIV negative and only in for respite care.   Rather withdrawn, quiet except for bursts of temper, with her crossed eyes and crippled legs she seemed content to remain in a corner.   When it came to the big treat, taking the children to the sea for the first time, Gaby was not thought of as likely to benefit from it, but Kevin said he would be responsible for her and so she went.   We all had a marvellous day, but what a truly wonderful day Kevin and Gaby had together.   Their friendship developed, tentative at first like all good friendships, but Kevin won her confidence and although when they got to the seaside it was a long trudge down to the sea through the sand, somehow they made it.   No-one would have believed Gaby would not only get into the sea but right up to her armpits by the end of the day.   All due to Kevin's belief in her and his gentle coaxing.   Not only that, but by the time Kevin left she could count up to five in English and Romanian, and to see Gaby's face as she discovered through Kevin the ability to make music with the various percussion instruments was something those of us who witnessed it will never forget.   She called Kevin Doctor Kev, which of course was what he was, a doctor of music.

By this time the hospice was running at full capacity.   To keep these dying children clean and happy is a full time job, especially towards the end. Vasilica, a dear little girl, growing more feminine and beautiful each day, slowly lost the battle to stay alive and suffered heart congestion which made it hard for her to breathe.   For the last three weeks of her life she was handed from loving arms to loving arms, people giving up their precious free time to walk the hospice with her day and night. Denisa died too, such a little star, and we used to hear her singing to herself in her cot. And cots were beginning to be a problem. Even without George's help they were not standing up to the hammering they got as the children grew. So small beds had to be obtained and the fitter and larger children transferred.

*   *   *

Back at home at the start of 1994, I received a message saying "Don't leave it too long before coming to visit again as Alexandru is going down-hill." I was due out in May and felt I should not come out earlier as I had to time my visits to help sort the lorry deliveries. Perhaps God was being kind, as the nurse manager said; he died two weeks before I was due out, so at least I remember him still as a sturdy little boy, not the thin wan child he became. His mother had started to visit him and take him home, and on his last day he asked to see machinas. With the nurse manager driving and another girl cuddling him on her lap they drove him round the town to see the cars and lorries and then to his home where he died in his mother's arms later that night.

He is buried with his grandfather on the hillside overlooking the town and from it you can see the hospice. Many little graves are there both from the hospice and from the orphanage - all tended and looked after. Some of the girls find relief from their grief by writing poems about the children as they died. I treasure the one I was sent about Alexandru.

You said he was different, you knew straight
away
He found a place in your heart, his very first day.
You watched him so`closely at rest and at play,
He experienced such love, you showed him the
way.

You loved his wee sulks, his tantrums too
And they melted away as he spent time with
you.
His treasured possessions you supplied for him
too
A bag for his back, photos of his mum, him and
you.

You sent him wee gifts, the things he did need,
Clothes and machinas and books he could read,
Judy, he'd say and look ever so pleased.
His mum number two on that we're agreed.

You hoped you would see him, just even once
more.
Why couldn't he wait, you'll have asked for sure.
You hurt so within, there is pain, tears galore,
But nought can compare with what God has in
store.

Chapter 10

Albania, the Land the World Forgot
* * * * * * * * * *

I have been lucky. Like many other people I went out to Romania to give and I received much more. The children have taught me how to live life to the full, not to fear death so much and to enjoy the simple pleasures in life. I also discovered it was possible to make a difference in just one spot of misery in the world, but I must admit I had not bargained for trying to help to do it again, this time in Albania.

However, this was how I came to find myself face to face with a Kalashnikov. Unlike Romania, where one could hire a gun, then hire a man to hold it, and finally hire some bullets in case he had to use them, in Albania it all comes in one package and a very volatile one at that.

Albania's problems were similar in a way to Romania's. By 1944 it was fully in the hands of the communist party, led by a man called Hoxha. However, he gradually began to regard other communist states as being too lenient, even in the end China. He kept his country under a more repressive regime than any other communist country, and closing the borders, only allowed a very limited number of people permission to enter, and fewer to leave. People were imprisoned for painting pictures or composing music which he deemed against the state. Quite often these people lived, married, had children and died still in prison, their children automatically being imprisoned with them. Early in the 1970s Hoxha announced that religion of any sort was to be abolished. All religious books, pictures, and artefacts were to be brought into the streets and burnt on a certain day. Anyone found with anything even faintly religious after that would be, and was, shot.

In Albania as in Romania, land was collectivised, private property abolished, and every punitive measure that could be employed ensured the complete control of the people. Anyone found trying to escape from Albania, by swimming across to Corfu, for instance, was shot on sight. One man, I was told, had tried paddling across on a mattress, but it had become waterlogged, and the police patrol boat watched him drown. Another man built a raft and mounted an old lorry engine on the back, but also failed to reach safety.

Hoxha fed his people a diet of lies and fears about the capitalist countries waiting to invade Albania at the slightest chance. He passed a decree that everyone should contribute to the cost of the defence of the country by funding the building of nearly a million reinforced concrete pill boxes. Sometimes an attempt is made to chip away the concrete to get at the iron bars, but for the most part they just litter the countryside, monuments to one man's folly.

For anyone living in Britain it is difficult to grasp what it must be like to live in a country dominated by one man, with no access to any other information than that allowed by him, in constant fear of your life if, by even a blink of an eye, you deviate from the party line. It takes many years to break the habits of a lifetime and even begin to contemplate independent thought and action, as we have seen all too well in

Romania. There, a year after Ceaucescu's overthrow, a government official told me they were like headless chickens, and recently among the older people there were grumbles that at least under Ceaucescu they *got* half a bar of soap and some bread.

In Albania after the death of Hoxha in 1985, his widow continued to observe her husband's wishes (and guard her life style) for the running of his country, and the new leader Ramiz Alia was only forced to relax some of the rules when events in the rest of Eastern Europe, particularly the overthrow of Ceaucescu in Romania, started ripples of unrest through Albania. In 1990 Ramiz Alia started to announce various reforms, permission to travel abroad, a loosening of restrictions on religion, and made an attempt to start the handing back of land to the peasants. Not as easy as it sounds. In Romania, the great unwieldy tracts of land, bulldozed of every tree or recognisable landmark, are still being argued over and in some cases fought over by people who think they have a legitimate claim to some of it.

In the summer of 1991 more than 25,000 people tried to reach Italy by seizing ships moored in the Albanian port of Durres. I shall never forget the television pictures and newspaper reports of the rusting 9,000-ton ship Vlora, with more than 10,000 people on board. They clung all over the ship, someone said it looked like starlings roosting. People were even sitting round the edge of the funnel, some had been clinging to the masts for 12 hours, and every available foothold was taken. When they reached Italy many panicked at the thought of not being allowed to land, and jumped into the water. Hundreds of Italian police eventually herded everyone into a football stadium.

There they remained without food and water for

another night and day. Riots started, children became separated from their parents and people were trampled under foot. Eventually helicopters were sent to drop food into the stadium, but most of it was seized by gangs, and the women and children still got nothing. The second day the stadium was covered in mounds of excreta, with flies swarming on the filth. The refugees began to fight the police who opened fire. On the third day, residents of Bari, ashamed by what was going on, began to bring bags of food for the refugees, but by this time many of them had given up hope of their dream of a new life in the West, and were prepared to be shipped back to Albania. The hard core of 2,000 who were prepared to fight to the death to remain in Italy were eventually told they would be flown to a new life in Rome or Milan, only to find the planes actually took them back to Tirana in Albania.

All this began to alert people to the misery there must be in Albania, and Bill Hamilton, a correspondent with the BBC, uncovered and showed the world the really dreadful state of the children in the so-called hospitals for mentally ill children, doing for them what the Anneka Rice program had done for the Romanian orphanages. His book, "Albania Who Cares?" is still to my mind the most truthful and moving account written about the state of Albania and these children since Hoxha was overthrown.

After watching Bill's television News Report from the hospital in Shkoder the Executive Director of the charity "Feed the Children", David Grubb, wrote two poems:

THE HOME

The flies are always ready to play,
darting between darkness and silence and the
stench of scars.

The children hunch in remote coils of
desolation; they perch between stranded ideas,
dream junk, no longer remembering what
anything is meant to be.

There are no toys, no games, no names:
there is no colour.
Tides of torture relentlessly lap on crooked
dreams.

One boy stretches into space,
recoils, springs out again,
as if there were somewhere to fly.

In the same cold cage, two others squat,
frozen in despair, too tired even to rock,
to continue pecking at their chains.

THE ROOM

This is the sitting room. This is the room
Where we sit all day. This is the floor.
These are the walls. This is the window
Where there is no glass. This is the ceiling.
This is the useless radiator. This is the
place where the light bulb hung. This is
the door. It shuts. It is closed. There
is nothing either side. This is the sitting room.
The sitting down in silence room. The nothing

room.
The all life room.   The room where we are.
The room where we will remain.
This is the entire world.   This is the total
existence.
This is the no room.   The don't room.   The
cannot room.
The never ever room.   The will never room.
This is the sitting room.

No child should live like this, any more than a
child should die in a cot in Romania not knowing a
cuddle or a kiss, and David and I jumped at a chance to
visit Albania with the charity to see what could be done
to help.   Right at the very start of our visit an official,
when asked what help was needed for the disabled and
mentally deficient children of his country, said they did
not have any.   That turned out to be as chilling as
Ceaucescu's refusal to acknowledge AIDS in Romania.
As for the sick children we saw in the hospital in the
capital of Albania, Tirana, the wards were full of
children with diseases and infections that in this country
would just be an inconvenience, but without antibiotics
a lot would die, already weakened by malnutrition.
Many had gastro-enteritis. There were three premature
babies all together in an incubator which had broken
down months before, but the doctor said he felt better
for putting them in it.   In some hospitals if a woman
had just given birth and could not breast-feed her new
baby she had to go round the ward begging the other
mothers who could to help, as here not only were there
no bottles or teats but no milk either.
       Spurred on by the success of the hospice in
Romania it was decided by the charity that the best way

to help would be to build a modern children's hospital in Saranda. This town, placed as it is a short ferry ride from Corfu, would be cheaper and easier to get at than Tirana. Isolation had kept Albania free from AIDS, but when we visited the existing hospital in Saranda the children' s wards were very empty for a hospital caring for the needs of some 80,000 people. A severe flu-like illness had killed quite a number of children in the wards, and mothers were afraid to bring their children in.

Bits of cardboard filled in broken windows, because the glass factory, like most other industrial centres, had come to a halt. The cots were rusting and the open concrete brick heaters with glowing coils were truly frightening when the electricity cuts allowed them to be on. The one lavatory for the whole of the children's floor had a cistern over the hole in the ground but no water. A bucket of water did for washing syringes and hands. In spite of everything the doctors and nurses were plentiful and caring, and David was impressed by the standard of their training. "All we need are supplies", the director told us. A new custom-built children's hospital was something he dared not even dream about.

The usual crumbling blocks of flats climb the hill behind the port. Even when the water is turned on it does not have the power to reach much higher than the third floor. Pigs root among the rubbish and people squat on the broken pavements with a few bits and pieces in front of them hoping for a buyer. Sticking out like a sore thumb was an upright brand-new fridge/freezer beside an old lady. I learnt her son had managed to get to Corfu and had earned enough money to send it to her. As even if she had electricity for more than a couple of hours a day she could not afford to run it, and certainly had no means of getting food to go in it, she sat every day hoping for a buyer. She did not seem too despondent, as apparently she had got a very good price for the cardboard box it was packed in.

The hotel in Saranda was a palatial affair, all marble floors and dusty red plush curtains. Again it had a familiar air, as it was built for good party members and the high echelons of Hoxha's government to take holidays by the sea. I was used to the lack of water; if you missed the hour or two a day it was turned on it was just bad luck, and I had a torch for when the electricity did not come on. But there is a limit to the amount of food one can take in one's luggage, and the second evening there the hotel had run out of everything except wine and carrot jam - not a very gourmet combination.

However, luckily the chief engineer for the project had acquired some dynamite to blast out a flat area for the new hospital, and had used some surplus to requirements to go fishing. We started on the wine while he vanished home to fetch a fish. Then it was discovered that because the hotel had no food all the kitchen staff had quite sensibly gone home. So the engineer and the director of the local hospital took over the cooking of the fish. I just hope they are better at their jobs than they are as cooks! Half-cooked fish and carrot jam do not act much in the way of blotting paper for wine, and next day my eyebrows were already rather stiff. By the time I came face to face with the man with the Kalashnikov at the road block on our way back to Tirana, having my head blown off seemed quite a nice idea.

What really frightened me about him was his

look of total indifference. His was the sort of face I imagined cold-bloodied killers had. I felt he could kill me with no more trouble than swatting a fly. David and I had been left in the van while the rest of the party including the driver had been taken off to a concrete block house, from where I could hear heated voices and what sounded like the clap of fist on flesh. Not for the first time I wondered what I was doing, a grandmother of uncertain years, built more for the weekly battle in the local Sainsbury's. Thinking this reminded me I had a packet of jelly babies in my bag, and very carefully and slowly, keeping my bag in full view, I opened it and held sweets out through the window. There was a long pause, then the man's face changed like the sun coming out from behind a cloud. His grin exposed a mouthful of cracked and broken teeth but juggling with the Kalashnikov he managed to acquire a large handful of sweets. At that moment our driver appeared, dishevelled but smiling, escorted by a group of smartly dressed police and more men with guns, but all now beaming away. Behind them came the rest of the party and our Mr Fixit, our agent from Romania, smiling ruefully as he put back his wallet.

More road blocks followed, and Mr Fixit began to look worried. Apparently it was politic to get through the last ones before darkness fell, and Tirana was still quite some way off. It had taken us eight hours so far to cover 60 miles, through a countryside beautiful in its natural splendour and appalling in its poverty, described variously as the land of eagles, or the place the world forgot. It is a place where "women are the property of men, to be bought, sold and betrothed before birth". Where else in the world, I wonder, does a bridegroom get given a silver bullet during the wedding ceremony, symbolic of his right to shoot his wife should she try to leave him? It is a place of blood feuds, lasting generations, where even today men are trapped in their homes unable to go near a window or door knowing they are next in line for a vengeance killing.

Like other Balkan states Albania has been fought over and used as a pawn by many other stronger, richer and more powerful countries throughout the centuries, and this has left it with a mish-mash of cultures, religions, peoples and borders. It is a country not much bigger than Wales, mostly mountainous, with a fertile plain and a beautiful seaboard, and has a population of around three million, 50 per cent of them under twenty-one. About 70 per cent of the population are Moslem, the rest assorted Christians; there is a vocal ethnic Greek Orthodox minority, and Catholics and Baptists as well. For a country that declared itself the first official atheist state in the late 1960s the religious fervour since the overthrow of the Communist regime in 1991 seems in some cases associated more with the size and content of the latest aid lorry from the various churches than with their religious tracts. If so, again I would not blame them. You are never too old to learn in this life, and what I saw and experienced in Romania and then in Albania, taught me not to make judgements, especially not from the safety of my own fireside.

The scenery we passed through on our way to Tirana was stunning, with a dramatic back drop of snow-capped mountains most of the way. At one point we reached a desolate place with rusting "nodding donkeys" dotted over the landscape. I had seen these before in California, but there they were nodding busily away sucking up the oil. Here none of them were working and black oil oozed out of the ground. It was running down the hillsides into a river which was coated in black, like the small boys playing in it. They threw stones and lumps of oil at us, and I was glad I did not understand Albanian.

Eventually we reached Tirana, but by the time we had found the hotel all the food for the day had gone. By the next evening, after a day spent meeting various government officials to get the project under way, I must admit I was very hungry. So hungry, in fact, that when we were invited to supper at the house that Hoxha used as his own personal club I tucked into the first little dish that appeared in front of me with relish. It looked like rings of kalamari in a rather spicy sauce and was extremely chewy. Looking down the table I could see David was not tucking in with his usual enthusiasm for food, but the Romanian ambassador to Albania who was sitting on my left congratulated me on my appetite. "Not many of your countrymen like intestine," he said. This was followed by a plate of cold chips, rather undercooked, and I cannot for the life of me remember whether we had anything else. There was an awful lot of wine, and a great deal of "Kazua", my only Albanian word, which means "Cheers".

Our visit to Albania had been brief but sufficient to see how much a new children's hospital with up-to-date equipment was needed. On the way to the airport next day we saw an avenue of trees that were only stumps, and small boys were hacking away at them for chips of firewood. And there was a man digging a 10-acre field with a small shovel. Waiting to say goodbye at the airport was the Deputy Minister of Health, who had cycled the eight miles from town to see us off. "We have had so many promises of help," he said, "Forgive me if I doubt you will come back, but I dare not hope."

As we took off down the runway I looked out of the window and there was an old woman with a flock of sheep waving her stick and shaking her fist at us, while the sheep scattered in all directions. I admit that when I reached Heathrow I felt I wanted to do as the Pope does and kiss the tarmac! There was going to be a lot to organise and do if the Albanian children's hospital was going to be built. Every nail, bag of concrete, brick and plank would have to be brought in from elsewhere.

Chapter 11

Women - There's No Pleasing Them
* * * * * * * * * *

However, there was still much to do in Romania, and much as I wanted to be in the two places at once I felt I was of more use if I concentrated on the hospice. This still needed to be funded. Disposable nappies were used at the rate of around 700 a week, even with some of the children becoming potty-trained. So it was back to the fund-raising, a job which, with the best will in the world, became harder and harder. I had to think up as many different ways of extracting money and goods from people as I could. There are many appeals for good causes in our own country, never mind abroad, and everyone has some reason for supporting a particular one. Perhaps a relative has died from cancer, or a friend is blind or deaf, and then there are all the animal charities, always well supported. There is no doubt that media coverage of places like Romania and Albania helped, but then it's on to somewhere else, Bosnia, Rwanda or China. Good news does not seem to be so newsworthy either, and after a bad report on goods going astray, or the business of the couple who were imprisoned for trying to smuggle a baby out of Romania, it always needed a fresh effort to convince people to part with their money or goods all over again. In a back-handed way it helped when I was able to tell them stealing begins at home. After a local newspaper appeal raised a whole lorry load of nappies, these were packed into the lorry and left overnight in a so-called secure compound before leaving for the docks. Next morning it had gone; according to the police the lorry off to the continent where there is a ready market for lorries, and the nappies to the nearest car boot sale.

Of course there are rogues and robbers in Romania, and even more in Albania, but in a way they seem more honest! Our Romanian Mr Fixit told me he once worked for Moslems - "Then I was a good Moslem," he said. "Under the communists I was a good communist, and now I work for a vicar I am a good Christian". And at least if the things were stolen in Romania they would reach someone in need.

The business of whether the illegal adoption of children was right was more difficult to answer. People here were saying surely anything was better than leaving them in the orphanages. As usual it is not so simple. When I first started travelling out to Romania the passengers on the plane were divided up between the usual business-men, groups of skiers in winter, tourists going to the Black Sea resorts in summer, groups of aid workers, and anxious-looking couples holding hands and sitting in silence or looking through folders of papers. They were the ones desperate for a child, unable to see an end to the waiting list for one at home, who were prepared to do or pay anything to make their dream of being parents come true. At first they were able to go to an orphanage, and with very little in the way of bureaucracy, choose a child to bring back. Then the trouble started. Children who had been kept in cots and become institutionalised were sometimes too traumatised and damaged to respond. They had severe behavioural problems, or had been given a certificate of health and then on being examined in Britain were found to be HIV positive. Some couples could not cope, and the children were abandoned all over again in this country. It is no wonder that the Romanians, coming under severe criticism from abroad, should tighten up control of the adoption procedures, especially after a rumour that paedophiles were taking advantage of the slack system. The paper-work has mounted, the regulations pile up and the penalties are severe for the illegal trade in children, but is it any wonder?

It's the same with donated goods. Running a charity shop I soon learnt to dread some of the black plastic bags handed over with the demand that I guarantee everything would go out. No-one seemed to work out that second hand clothing had to have a good length of life left in it to make it viable to be sent on a lorry costing £2,000. Little jumpers and T-shirts tend to become oblong after a few washes, vests go hard round the neck, and babygrows become thin. Out-of-date medicines and food, although we know they are probably still effective, are not good enough for dying children. Would we honestly want our children, when they are ill, to be given such stuff? Again the Romanian authorities got tired of lorry loads of unsuitable, sometimes dirty clothing, and out-of-date stuff being unloaded on them. New regulations stated all clothing had to have a certificate of dry cleaning, or they were to be new, and all medicines and goods had to be well in date. Another barrage from people who said they ought to be thankful for anything!

Shortly after the new decree came into force I was back out at the hospice to help unload a container sent all the way from Australia. First of all we had to pay rather a lot to have it transported from the port, and then it arrived complete with its own personal

Romanian customs official who was to supervise the unloading and checking of the contents. The charity had been assured all was good stuff, and we would be pleased. In temperatures reaching the 100s we started, the official making himself comfortable on the top of the steps in the shade. Without exception all the drugs and medicines were out-of-date and had to be burnt under the eagle eyes of the official. This had to be done in our incinerator, which was a skip used to burn the nappies and which smouldered day and night at the back of the hospice. All we managed to find a use for were some paper towels. There were some boxes of syringes and catheters which would have been more suitable for horses, not children.

As night fell we bribed the official with a bottle of brandy to go away and not put in an official complaint, and promised it would all be burnt. The night watchman, aged 76, and I spent a romantic moonlit night pushing a wheelbarrow up the slope to the incinerator and throwing in the rubbish. All went fairly well until it got to the phials of injectable drugs. These were easy enough to throw onto the really hot fire we had going by then, but started to explode and shoot glass all over the place. It sounded as though war had broken out, woke all the dogs of the neighbourhood up, and reduced both the night watchman and myself to hysterical laughter as we armed ourselves with dustbin lids to fend off the exploding glass and continued to hurl handfuls of the wretched phials onto the fire. Having promised the man everything would be burnt by morning I did not put it past him to come and check. We would have been fresh out of brandy, as the night-watchman and I needed something for dutch courage. I am pleased to say that the large plastic syringes were extremely useful, they made the most marvellous water pistols for the children, and many a battle took place on the flat roof of the hospice during the summer.

My main job at the hospice was to try to keep the stores in some sort of order. This was easier said than done. There were four main storerooms, all far too small - when is a storeroom ever big enough? The baby store had everything from baby food, shampoos, bubble baths, lotion, wet wipes, bibs and of course nappies. The clothing store had all the winter and summer clothing for the children and the bedding, and of course nappies. The household store had soap, soap powder, bleach, plastic sacks, brooms, mops, buckets, and lavatory cleaners, and the dry goods store had porridge, powdered milk, pasta, cereals, jam, tins - mostly beans - and nappies. Then there was the medical store room with the disposable gloves, plastic aprons, syringes, needles, sutures, swabs, dressings, disinfectants - and nappies! The nappies got everywhere, even in the mortuary. Each make of nappy seems to have a different system of labelling for size, some by weight, some by age, and then of course there are the ones for boys and the ones for girls. All very different from my day and very muddling for a grandmother with grandsons. When I lent a hand at nappy-changing time up on the wards the girls would chant "Teddies to the front" or "Teddies to the back" as I was handed another little one.

When a lorry arrived at the hospice up to 10 tons of stores had to be unloaded and found a space for in a very short time. A lot of the stuff would not be labelled or be in black plastic bags, and for obvious reasons all the goods had to be locked away somewhere secure even if unsorted, so when I opened up the storerooms it could be quite daunting.   However, the storerooms were all in the basement, nice and cosy in the winter if they were not flooded, as the laundry was down there as well, but it could get awfully hot in the summer.   I used to get up around 6 a.m then, and take my first cup of coffee out into the yard.   It was a lovely time of day with the sun coming up over the Danube, and cows and pigs beginning to emerge from their sheds, usually one or two to a house.   They all seemed to know exactly what to do, and walked slowly past the hospice out to the fields on the edge of the town for the day, coming back in the evening.   I would put in a quiet hour down in the basement and then come back up around 7.30 - 8.00 to frighten the life out of the Romanian staff coming on duty late.   The cleaning ladies in particular had to be flushed out of their changing rooms around that time.   None of them bore me any resentment, either for chasing them around or keeping a tight rein on the issuing of soap or J-cloths.   The washing machines were usually going full pelt, and would continue rumbling away till dusk.   The lady in charge and I used to compare varicose veins over a cup of coffee around four in the afternoon.   She certainly had the edge on me with veins, but I reckon my bunion was bigger.

There is something extremely satisfying in creating order out of chaos, even though I used to finish up never wishing to see another black plastic bag or bulging cardboard box full of junk ever again.   Word would get round that I was down there, and along would come a little procession of carers with the children one at a time to see if there were a pair of shoes a size bigger, or a special dress for a birthday.   Little Elena was going home for the weekend, so thin and weak she could hardly stand, but knowing exactly what colour dress she wanted and a cardigan to match, please. Barbara who had brought her down also asked for another dress, as pretty and frilly as possible, with matching lace tights. "Her mother wants her to die at home, and needs them to keep by her to lay her out". I never got used to it.

Valentina was a difficult customer. Having had every box of shoes out on the ground and sorted through she finally decided on the first pair she tried on. However, after a visit by Daniella who returned to the ward with a different pair, *that* pair was what she had really wanted. Daniella being the last person to part with anything, especially a pair of patent shoes with pink bows on even if it turned out they were very uncomfortable to wear, all the shoe boxes had to be gone through again to prove there were no others just like that.

Daniella is a story in herself. Reading the medical notes that come in with the children is like dipping into a horror story. Not only are they all HIV positive, but have things like TB, recurring pneumonia, chickenpox and shingles, bronchitis, abscesses, thrush, bad ears, decaying teeth and some have stiff limbs or suffer fits. And there are many more who are spastic or mentally retarded. But when I first saw Daniella when she had been undressed I had to shut myself in one of the bathrooms to get over the shock. There I was found by Simon, a tough young lad who considered himself the British answer to Michael Schumacher when behind the wheel of any vehicle, ambulance or mini-bus, and had the wrecks to prove it. "Brace up old girl," he said, putting his arms round me and giving me a hug. "This is just what we are here for." I admit I was terrified to touch her in case her sticks of legs and arms broke. She had a huge head, with the skin stretched tightly across the face. I could not see how she could still manage to survive, and was not surprised to hear she had only been given three weeks to live. She was still alive two weeks later when I left for home, and I expected to hear daily of her death, and I must admit I hoped for a speedy end for her.

Not a bit of it; by the time I was out again six months later she had put on weight, was sitting up and demanding attention from everyone. She was extremely choosy even then about the colour of her clothes, and woe betide anyone who crossed her. Not that anyone did, she was spoilt by everyone. Her hair grew black and curly, she started to stomp about and put on so much weight that they tried to put her on a diet. Imperious and demanding, Daniella is now 12 years old and still going strong. Her picture taken when she came in and then a year later said it all, and by showing it to people here it raised thousands of pounds from people who might otherwise have said, why bother with dying children? I was taken to task by one woman for showing the pictures as apparently I should have asked Daniella's permission, otherwise it was an abuse of her rights. Daniella has only to see someone with a camera and she elbows all other children out of the way, adjusting her curls and shouting "Pose, pose", but I was so taken aback at the fairly virulent attack by this lady I made enquiries as to the position. Apparently all the children who have no parents who come into the hospice are formally under the guardianship of Dr Matusa, and she can give permission on behalf of the child.

Dr Matusa also cannot help getting deeply involved with the children, both in her hospital and at the hospice. They all love her ward rounds and cling on to every part of her they can reach. Not only does she have to cope with the children's deaths, she has the task of telling parents their child has AIDS, then perhaps testing the parents and finding at times that either the mother, father or another child in the family is HIV positive. She has around 600 on her books as outpatients, and 200 at a time on her crowded wards. With very little extra money or help available she has still managed to slow the death rate down from 50 a month to about five, but has been faced, as the hospice has, with the problem of what to do with children who are obviously going to live longer and need not spend the rest of whatever life is left to them on the wards of a hospital. As sponsorship and money becomes available she is trying to set up houses for them with house-mothers, so that they can experience some sort of normal home life, but it is a slow business, made slower by lack of funds. She works seven days a week and hardly takes any time off for a holiday, not only running her department in the hospital, overseeing these homes, writing up her research, communicating with AIDS specialists all over the word and attending seminars, but trying to raise money as well.

She and her colleague from the Central Hospital, Liliana Popescu, another kindly and caring doctor with special responsibilities for the hospice, did take the day off when I was out there in the summer of 1994. Together with my friend Christine, who ran the local charity shop and had come out to help sort another huge pile of deliveries, we all went on a trip along the coast. Mile after mile of Romanian Benidorm. Sandy beaches as far as the eye could see, with what must have been 200 hotels all along the edge of the Black

Sea, backed by a road, each group called after jewels, or Greek gods, or composers or minerals. It was quite extraordinary seeing the hundreds of people, beach umbrellas, ice-cream stalls. Romania has a coast of about 50 miles, and makes the most of every inch.

We stopped at a museum of Roman remains, beautifully laid out, with marvellous reproductions of Roman glass for sale. In one shop we went into I even saw a Barbara Cartland novel, in Romanian. The shops were an eye-opener. In 1991 they were little better than the front room of a house, with a trestle table for a counter. Sometimes the only thing on it would be two or three packets of chewing gum, each piece for sale separately, and half a dozen cigarettes. A few blackened carrots in the winter and a few flowers in the summer, and somewhere I have a photograph of an entire shop with just one single item in pride of place, a packet of soap powder.

Most of the hotels, I was told, had been built during the communist regime to reward those workers who had toed the line with cheap holidays. The grumble nowadays is that with the influx of foreign tourists the hotels had priced themselves out of the local market. Certainly Romania has been quick to catch up with the rest of Europe. I am told that there is a McDonald's and a Pizza take-away in Bucharest now, and certainly down below the hospice when I was last out there was an ice-cream parlour, well attended by the children and carers during the summer, sporting striped parasols and white plastic chairs and tables.

Food was a bit of a problem for the hospice in the early days. Not so much for the children, but for the carers and helpers. Our young seem to panic if they are out of reach of a take-away, and expect their meat and vegetables to come in neat plastic-covered containers. When the Paschal lamb arrived in the back of the minibus one Easter, bleating gently, I hastily helped the chef bundle it into an empty garage, where it spent a happy night with plenty of grass and water. The new chef, as thin as the previous one was fat, but much more ready to please if he could only make head or tail of the orders given him, seemed to understand my pleas to keep the presence of the lamb a secret from the carers, and to despatch it quietly and discreetly in the early hours of Easter Sunday. I had forgotten that early to Matica meant around 9 o'clock, and that is when I saw him next morning, standing on the steps of the hospice having his first cigarette.

With a happy "Buna dimineata" (good morning) he brandished a very large knife at me and drawing it across his throat shouted "Baa-baa finish in a minute" or words to that effect. Well, I enjoyed the lamb at lunch. In vain I had tried to tell the girls that really the way animals were kept and killed in Romania beat our system hands down. The pig-killing day in the New Year I must admit was pretty noisy and gory. They were brought out of their sheds, laid on trestles, and in with the knife. Of course I could remember it used to be the way in this country, and tried to explain it must be much better than living the sort of life they do here, being loaded onto lorries and driven long terrifying hours across country to abattoirs where they are kept overnight within smelling distance of the killing sheds, however quickly they are dispatched in the end. This little homily only had the effect of turning most of the girls into instant vegetarians.

To start with there were plenty of donated tins and packets which came out on the lorries, and many and varied were the meals, especially when some of the labels had come off. But eventually the kitchens at the hospice began to cope, and meals had to be taken in its dining room, leaving space on the lorries for more pressing supplies. The children were fed first, and it was quite a test of character to post a mush of mashed potato and green peas in one end, followed by rice pudding, wipe it up again from the other end, and then go down shortly afterwards to face a similar menu in the dining room. However, as the old saying goes "Hunger makes a good sauce".

It was just as well that the girls did not find out some of the other little problems with the food down in the basement.   As part of my self-inflicted duties I inspected the food stores whenever I went out to the hospice, together with the chef.   Matica, having been promoted from assistant chef on the departure of his boss, was very anxious to make a good impression. Shortly after his elevation and my arrival we were due to have a visitation by some VIPs from head office. They would be arriving late and not need a meal that night, but an early breakfast.   Matica, in his endeavour not to be late on parade, decided to sleep at his post, and when I went over to the kitchens early next morning to check he had arrived, there he was snoring away on the kitchen table, using the clean table cloth I had put out the night before as a sheet.   He seemed quite hurt at my lack of appreciation for his self-sacrifice, especially as he pointed out he had carefully removed his boots. Given the state of his socks and feet I was still not pleased, and it confirmed him in his long held suspicion that women were the same the world over, never satisfied.

It was confirmed even more when we had a little

falling out over the temperature in the chill room. I was telling him it must be turned down when I noticed some brown specks on a side of beef. When I pointed them out to him he leant over and tenderly brushed them, and the ash falling from his cigarette, onto the floor. I realised they were mouse droppings, and then to my horror discovered them in the sugar bin. Smiling sweetly he waved his arms around, "No problem - Romania many many mice". And sure enough there were, especially in the food store room, making nests in racks full of empty jars.

Keeping this information from the female staff I enlisted as many of the male nurses, doctors, and lorry drivers as I could find and we started clearing out. It reminded me of the fairground game of throwing a ping-pong ball into jars. They always seemed to bounce out and you could never get the gold fish offered as a prize. The mice leapt out of one jar into another as fast as they were cleared, and some of the men were just as afraid of the mice as some of the girls. If one jumped in their direction instead of catching it or stamping on it as the others were doing they squeaked as much as the mice and leapt out of the way. Someone had the bright idea of getting one of the yard dogs down as he looked as though he had a bit of terrier in him, but confused by all the shouting and being allowed indoors he bit someone's ankles and had to be removed growling fiercely.

The problem was still being addressed when I left, but Matica assured me the temperature in the meat store would be turned down. On my next visit out to the hospice and subsequent inspection he proudly showed me a side of beef, certainly very cold as there was a frozen mouse stuck to the side. I did not need a dictionary to translate his conversation with the night watchman when I passed them having a cigarette together later in the day - "There's no pleasing them" - on which they were both heartily agreed.

The night watchman had troubles of his own. Being rather elderly, as I have said, he was inclined to doze off during the night in his little shed. Having been discovered and warned several times by the nurse manager, and swearing he was on guard to every sound, Sheila decided to teach him a lesson. The new ambulance was parked in the yard and needed a very sharp eye kept on it. During the night she removed all the wheel hubs, spare wheel, wing mirrors and even unscrewed the lights while he provided music as she worked with his snores.

As well as the night watchman there were any number of dogs from two to 10, including the fresh crop of puppies, on the pay roll. Every piece of property in Romania has its dog, and the bigger the property the more dogs to the square foot. They are tremendous bark machines, and somehow know friend from foe, in spite of the constant coming and going of different people. But another of my tasks was to try and limit the number, for hygiene reasons apart from anything else, and I got very tired of having to sound the death knell on the puppies. When I discovered on a visit that there was a vet on the staff of carers I was delighted, and asked if he could spay the current female and her puppy. To give him his due it hardly took any nagging to get him to agree, and the visiting Romanian doctor was only too eager to assist. I had not bargained for the fact that they decided the only suitable place to undertake the operation was in my clothes store in the basement, and expecting some strong opposition they waited until I went on a visit to Bucharest. I suppose it could have been worse, the blood stains on the walls mixed in with the marks where I had squashed flies, and they had at least cleaned the floor up for me.

Having got into the swing of things the vet decided to delouse and worm the pup and her mother a week or so later. This time the operation took place in the yard, with a large audience of fascinated Romanians. Supplying a baby bath from the store room I joined them to see how it should be done. Willing girls filled the bath with nice warm water and the special shampoo, and the poor trembling dog was given her dose of worming mixture and lowered gently into the water. It was then the vet made his one and only mistake. Lulled into a false sense of security by the lack of fight in the dog, he turned to pick up the soap. With a huge lunge, which by the soaking they got must have deloused many of the audience, the dog shot off yelping, out of the yard, and could be heard heading for Constanta, followed by her puppy. As far as I know neither has been seen since.`

I was lucky enough to have made friends with the Domestic Manager's family who lived in the next street. His wife Veta was an excellent cook and on their little patch of garden they grew more fruit and vegetables than a full-scale market garden. They also had various animals living under, in and around the house. The kitchen was always warm and cosy in the winter and nothing delighted Veta more than for me to drop in and visit her and the grandma, with translations being provided by the eldest daughter who worked hard to keep up with the chat. One day I went to sink down gratefully on a seat by the stove when the cushion under me moved violently and a cat shot out, under that was a box with six tiny newly-hatched chickens being brooded by the cat! There was always something small and new to cuddle, either a kitten, or a lamb or a goat. Sometimes only the grandma was there, and unable to communicate in words we would just sit, near the fire in the winter, or under the grape arbour with the breeze off the Danube in the summer. I would always return to the hospice refreshed in more ways than one.

The variety and amount of food they seemed to have was an eye-opener. Sturgeon from the Danube, pork, veal, lamb or goatmeat from their own animals; tomatoes, melons, grapes, courgettes in the summer, potatoes, carrots, turnips and beetroot in the winter. And of course washed down by grandad's home-made wine. I felt this needed more work on it. It was cloudy, earthy, and gave you a splitting headache after the first glass, only cured by a second or a third. Even more lethal was the tsuica, a clear liquid that climbed out of the glass and was treated with caution even by the Romanians. As far as I could make out it was made from anything left over, but from exactly what was beyond the daughter's power of translation. When the main airport at Otopeni was given a face-lift, and a duty free shop installed, what should I see there but bottles of the stuff for sale labelled Dracula, an extremely apt name.

George and Veta's family lived well because they had been lucky. Ceaucescu had already earmarked their town for "redevelopment". Blocks of flats were built around the edge of what was a village, and people who had lost their homes and smallholdings from other areas were moved in, including a large quantity of gypsies, hated by the local people as troublemakers and thieves. The population doubled from 15,000. The next part of the programme was to be the demolition of the little houses like Veta's and George's, with the loss of their little bit of land and an end to their independence. Work was due to start after the Christmas of 1990, and the Grandma had taken to her bed and turned her face to the wall, determined to die before she was turned out and her family home destroyed. Luckily for them all, Ceaucescu's overthrow came just in time. The grandma made a full recovery and was able to teach me to make various Romanian dishes, and to show me the contentment to be found in a way of life without many of the modern trimmings.

Veta taught in the school I could see below the hospice, a decaying building swarming with children, and she invited me down to see round it. There are over 400 children, the younger ones attending in the mornings and the older ones in the afternoon. The lady in charge of the playground was armed with a large stick, but seeing the way the little ones cuddled up to her it was obviously more for show than use. Every classroom we visited the children stood up when we came in and wished us good morning, delighted to try out their English. One class showed me their pictures, another one put on a little musical entertainment, and another one acted out a Romanian fable for me. As they did not know I was coming I was most impressed. Without even the basics of enough paper and pencils, and having to share much-thumbed and out-of-date text books, I think schools here in the UK would be proud if their children reached the same standards. Russian used to be the first language after Romanian, now it's English, French or German.

I was invited into the staff room at break time, but there was a slight hiatus as there was no coffee or tea left. But someone produced a bottle of tsuica and we all toasted England, Romania, Education, Children, each other, the downfall of all officials, the Ministry of Education in particular; in fact it was just like some of the British school staff rooms I have visited, except that here, as it was winter, the staff kept on their tall fur hats at all times.

All of this was a welcome break from the work at the hospice. I have the greatest admiration for the young people who go out from Britain and Ireland and give up their time to work out there. One of the unexpected bonuses was the friendships formed with some of the girls, who kept me in touch with all the news when I had to come back home. They would have given up anything from three months to a year to go out and work, just for their board and lodging and a small amount of pocket money. However rewarding the work, it was still very hard physically and emotionally and a long way from home. It is also potentially lethal. I was known affectionately by them as the Biddy, and not so affectionately by some as the bossy Biddy! I must admit I did find sharing a bedroom hard at times. Most of them seem unable to function unless their space is a tip, which is all right until you try and share a small wardrobe and a chest of drawers with two of them.

I should not really grumble, after my first two visits I did at least get a bed to myself. A new experience for me, but apparently quite a usual thing among impoverished students, especially student nurses, was "hot-bedding", a very expressive term. As the night staff get out of their beds the day staff get in! On a visit to Bucharest three of us had to share a small double bed for the night in bitterly cold weather. The two youngsters kindly insisted the ageing biddy should sleep in the middle. Unfortunately during the night each of them in turn pulled the covers further their side of the bed, not only causing a draught but giving me what could have been a friction burn under my chin as the bristly blanket see-sawed to and fro. However, if you are tired enough lying flat is a joy.

While the young could spare more time I had to come home after three or four weeks each visit. David was very understanding, and coped extremely well but it was not fair to leave him on his own for too long, and the family began to complain that I was never there when wanted for baby-sitting. I remembered the broad hints to my three sons about getting married and starting in on providing me with grandchildren, and I felt guilty. I seemed to be leading two separate lives and I was finding it difficult. When I was at the hospice I was wondering what was happening at home, and when I was at home I was worrying about the children and carers at the hospice.

Cash flow for the hospice was still needed, and having run or helped to run over 150 events locally I was running out of ideas and steam. I was beginning to lose the ability to be tactful. If someone gave a lavish lunch in aid of the charity, but more to impress their friends than raise a decent amount, I told them so. At some events run by well-meaning people the only thing they made any money on was the raffle, after they had taken out all their expenses. I was proud of the fact that all the events I had run had cost nothing to put on; by dint of bullying and nagging, venues and food were sponsored or free, and my housekeeping stood the cost of stamps and telephone calls, and I expected the same from others.

Not only did people begin to avoid me in Sainsbury's, but it was felt that it was all right for me, I had a husband in a good job to fall back on for funds. A fair comment, but I was driven on by knowing how much we all really have in this country, and how desperate and urgent was the need of the children. With the best will in the world it is very difficult if you have not been out and seen this need for yourself. Which was why, when my friend Christine from the charity shop came back from her first visit, she decided to get a lorry up herself to get there by Christmas with as many of the things she saw needed as possible, and everything to make it a really special Christmas for the children, and for all the people, Romanian and British, at the hospice. After all, as she said, for some of the children it would be the only Christmas they would know.

The generosity of people in this country, especially when they have confidence that the money and goods will reach the intended destination, never ceases to amaze me. When the lorry set off at the beginning of December it was bulging with goodies. Forty boxes of biscuits and sweets for the Romanian staff, scented soap, lotions and perfumes for the girls, toys, colouring books, crayons, and of course sweets for the children, Christmas puddings, cakes, crackers, balloons, Coca-Cola and every available nook and cranny packed with packets of disposable nappies. Even some re-conditioned bikes and trikes for the children who could manage them in readiness for summer.

One particular item I was particularly pleased to have got onto the lorry. I had been given over 50,000 cod liver oil capsules, 200 to a bottle, but with only two weeks "use by" left. I knew Dr Matusa's hospital in Constanta was always in need of these capsules for the sick children, especially during the winter, but I also knew the Romanian authorities would not allow them in with such a short expiry date. Ringing the pharmaceutical company was easy, finding the right person to talk to and explain the problem less so, but finally I got someone to issue a certificate extending the date by six months. I also got a certificate from David, and he put all his letters after his name. I was quite pleased with the official-looking result, until I realised I still had the problem that the date was firmly on the capsule bottles and would cause trouble, especially for the drivers at the border. Luckily the previous week I had passed the premises of a company who packed tablets, and the raw materials were delivered in large white plastic buckets with lids. These buckets appeared to be standing idle, and proved quite easy to get my hands on, especially when I showed the bewildered storeman a picture of Daniella. Then it was back down to the charity shop and for all hands to open and empty each separate bottle of 200 into the buckets. How is it that child-proof tops to bottles should prove just as OAP-proof? It took three of us two and a half days, but we did it.

The inevitable question - will it all get there? In this case there was no doubt in our minds as the lorry was driven by two Metropolitan Police officers from the motorway squad. Owing to the camaraderie which exists among groups of professionals in the same line of business the world over, there was no problem at each of the many borders they had to cross. No pilfering or back-handers were expected or allowed. Should things have got tough they had their uniforms with them, along with the Father Christmas outfits. To save money they slept, ate and brewed up in the cab. Although it was only the first week in December snow was already falling when they got to the hospice after a fairly rough six days' hard driving, but like everyone else, they were completely overcome by the sight of the children. Christmas came early there and why not. The trikes and bikes were already being pedalled up and down the corridors before the police left, and lovely photos could go up in the shop to show people yes - it did all get there.

One of the most financially rewarding ways of raising money was to give talks to clubs, schools and groups, backed up by lots of photos of the children. No costs were involved, just the effort of going along and telling people about the children. For me it was getting more and more painful to do, especially during the run up to Christmas that year as 10 more children died, one after the other. Some I did not know, but most I did. As I talked about them I could see them clearly in my mind's eye.

For instance there was Skinny Petru, so called because he was so thin when he came in, and lost even more weight at the end until I could not believe a child could become so thin and last so long. While I was out at the hospice in the summer he had gone missing from the playground and no-one could find him. At first it was even feared that being so skinny he could have squeezed under the gate, or fallen through one of the gratings. A full-scale search was mounted by every available person, inside and outside the buildings. He was found quietly and contentedly playing with the contents of my handbag in my bedroom. He had applied the lipstick fairly generously, and the hand lotion, and was just starting on the powder. His tendency to prefer girls' dresses could I suppose have put him at a disadvantage if he had made old bones, but he was a delight to know and always made a comment if he thought your hair looked especially nice, or admired your earrings. Then there was dear Costel, growing up into such a responsible boy, caring for all the children in his ward, making sure no-one was left out of games or missed hand-outs of sweets if they were too poorly to leave their beds. Climbing into Toady's cot to have a chat if he was feeling too breathless to get out. Costel fought hard to stay alive, but after a succession of illnesses, including recurring and severe bouts of pneumonia, he suddenly seemed to become tired of life, especially after his special girl-friend Vasilica died, and he just slipped quietly away, mourned by many.

Then there was Jean Paul, another long-term inmate, who went back to Constanta Hospital to see if the quality of his life could be improved, but suddenly died. Extremely handicapped, unable to sit unaided or feed himself, it was my job to feed him and another severely handicapped child when I could spare time from the stores.

I have to confess that I am the sort of person the BBC radio programme "Does he take sugar?" was thought up to educate. In my own defence I have never had much to do with mentally or physically handicapped people and they make me feel nervous, mostly in case I inadvertently upset them. However, as long as I kept the spoon full and in and out of Jean Paul's mouth all seemed well. Otherwise he made deep grunting noises which sounded very threatening. He had teeth like a shark's, one eye seemed to look at you and the other didn't, and his arms flailed about uncontrollably. Worst of all he always had thick green mucus flowing copiously from his nose, and jerked his head away growling furiously if you tried to wipe it. Inevitably it would get mixed with lunch and then spat all over me when I tried to give him a drink. The other little one, Ouana, had a permanent smile on her face and although brain-damaged and "out with the fairies" as one helper used to say, would steadily and tidily chomp her way through lunch, unlike her neighbour on the ward, Sunita. Sunita had a very unpleasant habit of constantly regurgitating her food, a habit she had developed it was thought from being kept in a cot for years with nothing to play with or anything to look at except the walls of the room she was kept in. She would only take milk, not solids, and would get through two or more bottles at a time, then sit and post her hand down her throat at intervals. Her hair and clothes would become soaked and smelly in a very short time, however frequently she was changed and washed.

When I went up onto the wards on my last visit to the hospice I metaphorically rolled up my sleeves to do battle with Jean Paul, thinking to myself perhaps he was my own personal little cross to bear and I must try and hide my dislike for the task and get on with it, but at first I could not see him anywhere. Then to my amazement I saw him sitting on a little chair up at a table and feeding himself without any help. Thrusting his mug at me with the same old grunt I fetched him some water. Snatching it away he fixed me with one of his eyes as I bent over him and suddenly flung the contents all over me, then almost threw himself off the chair laughing. I am quite sure he was getting his own back on me for all the injustices and indignities he had suffered at my hands, and I must admit I was looking forward to continuing our acquaintance next time I went out, but it was not to be.

One after the other, then, coming up to that Christmas in 1994, the children died. I never seemed to have time to recover from the first painful grief of one death before I had news of the next. If a child or close relative dies here in this country there is usually someone close who can share the grief with you, even friends who have known the person, but with the carers and helpers scattered throughout Britain and Ireland it was very difficult. Friends did their best, and it was not their fault they got a bit fed up. I am sure other people have been told to "pull themselves together", "time heals", "count your blessings", and all the other well-meaning clichés. And so the talks, although bringing in the donations, became an added burden, as people loved to see photos of the children, but so many I had were now of children who had died.

I found I could not give the same talk each time, but had to tailor it to the audience. No way could I add to the worries of primary school children by dwelling on the plight of the Romanian children. Our own are pressurised every day by television and school about the environment, the cruel way their food is produced, the sad plight of various endangered species, the homeless and the less fortunate. It was lovely to attend something like a Harvest Festival when I could tell them how their strange gifts of disposable nappies, Milupa-type drinks and Early Learning plastic toys would be used, but my pre-talk nerves were not helped by headmistresses telling me to "give it to them strong, they all have wealthy parents or too much"; or the vicar at one assembly saying before it started he would be most interested as to how I was going to tackle the question of death with the children, as even he found it difficult. It seems to be the last taboo in our society, but in fact children seem to accept it as long as you leave it to them to ask the questions. When it got to the sixth-formers I certainly tried to explain the dangers of catching HIV, although at my age and upbringing I found it difficult to say "condom" without blushing. At one conference on the transmission of infectious diseases I had been asked to put up a small exhibition, and was given a table opposite people who, without my glasses, seemed to be handing out free samples of little square packets of single After Eights. Except these seemed to be new ones in different flavours, as I could hear raspberry or chocolate flavour being bandied about. I meant to go across and collect my own free samples but when I mentioned it to the girl from the next table and asked if she would like me to get her any, she kindly put me right, that they were condoms, which reduced us to giggles for the rest of the day every time she caught my eye.

For the groups of elderly people I found I had to be extra careful in my talk. Even the photos of the children reduced them to tears and myself with them, and they would give me far more than I was sure they could afford for "those dear little kiddies". Instead I bored them with various anecdotes of my journeys to and fro, the logistics of supplies, and usually had half of them asleep by the end, especially if it was an early afternoon talk and the heating was turned up.

The Rotarians and Round Tablers needed concrete facts and figures, the various women's groups and church groups wanted first-hand information about the children and no punches pulled. By the time Christmas 1994 was approaching I was doing an average of five talks a week. With illness in my immediate family my help was needed to look after my own grandchildren, four in all by that time. My middle son was thought to have cancer and rushed into hospital for investigations. Living as they do a three-hour journey away it was not easy. After an operation, thank goodness, he was pronounced clear, but then my eldest son was rushed into hospital with suspected meningitis the week before Christmas. Although it was a false alarm and they lived nearer, of course I was needed, and very glad to help. When Christmas finally arrived I was exhausted, and the inevitable happened, not helped by a six-hour stint carol singing for the charity. I had to take to bed in the New Year with a chest infection, and found I really did not ever want to get out of bed again. Even David was worried! The soldiers from the Lancers who went out to the hospice and had kept in touch, told me I was suffering from battle fatigue, aid workers told me it was called burn-out, others said it was compassion fatigue. Whatever it was I added to my troubles by falling out with the charity headquarters.

I became angry at what I thought was unnecessary waste, and they thought petty complaints, about using first-class stamps when second class would do, with letting the hospice run what I thought was too low on essential supplies like nappies and disposable gloves. I was nervous about the effect that the National Lottery would have, as people seemed to think we would automatically benefit from it, and I could stop badgering them for money. I got more and more cross at what I felt was a waste of money, although I know as charities get bigger administration needs rise. But when you have actually been the person to receive the widow's mite it is a great responsibility.

Enough was finally enough, and I had to stand back. No-one is indispensable and I had been extremely lucky. After all, it is not given to many people of my age, slightly past my sell-by date, to be part of something so concrete and immediate in alleviating suffering. I had shed more tears in those years than in the previous 60 odd, but I'd had more laughs as well. In the small hours of the morning (what a misnomer that is, as the hours are actually the longest in the 24, if you are awake) I still feel a failure, and that I have let the children down, but then I start to think about them, and the happy memories come flooding back. Aurelia, the day we brought her back from Constanta, and she asked to have her nails varnished and a little lipstick when she heard her favourite male nurse was back out. If she had lived she would have broken more hearts than Mike's... Toady, sitting with me on the hospice steps carefully sharing a pancake he had filched from the kitchens, down to the last crumb. At least he now knows what food is like in Heaven... My own Alexandru, and the sudden fierce kisses he used to give me, like my own grandsons, especially when I had just given him a new "machina"... The sight of the children asleep in their cots and beds when I sneaked up on the wards late at night... The feel of little Inouit's head under my chin as we had a sleepy rock together in the rocking chair after lunch.

I remember a lady saying "I hope those children are grateful to you" as she pushed a few coins rather reluctantly into my collecting box one day. The boot, madam, is definitely, but definitely, on the other foot.

* * * * * * * * *

Will I ever go back out to Romania? It is quite possible, the hospice is well supplied and due to be handed over to the Romanians, but I have been approached by Christine who has now started up her own lorry convoys, to go out with her as Dr. Matusa is having trouble with her storerooms in Constanta hospital, and they need a good sort through. "We'll go at the end of the summer, after the mosquitoes and before the snow," she says. "You'll love it." And I think she is right.

Chapter 12

At Last and Lastly
* * * * * * * * *

I have always had a struggle to cope with the long dark winter months, which are so often followed by a long dark and wet summer. My bones never feel dried out unless I can bask in hot sun, and I had tucked away that taste of sun in Corfu for future reference. When SAD (Seasonal Affective Disorder) was invented the word exactly described my condition, but by that time I had discovered my own cure, and it was not sitting under a light bulb.

As the boys grew holidays were still a chancy affair, mostly in damp tents in damp fields, but in 1976 my eldest son got pneumonia, and we had to find somewhere with guaranteed warmth for a couple of weeks that Easter. The holiday had to have sea (the boys), be cheap (David), and no tents (me). The hand of fate fell on Cyprus.

I knew nothing about the island at all, except that there had been trouble of some kind between Turks and Greeks, resulting in a division of the island, and my mother was quite convinced we would be shot by one side or the other.

After a four and a half hour flight we landed at midnight at Larnaca airport, not much more than a huddle of sheds, as the main airport at Nicoscia was out of bounds. I stepped onto the top of the aircraft steps to be met by a blast of hot air, so scented with orange blossom you could have cut it with a knife. A ceiling of stars in the blackest of skies, and a crescent moon lighting up the sea completed the picture. I felt I had come home, as though I knew this island, a most extraordinary feeling. Three grumpy tired boys and a fairly grumpy husband left me with no more time for such thoughts. The taxi driver, as large as his taxi was small, had a few English words, mostly of the "No problem" kind, but the 5 of us plus luggage were finally crammed in.

The main road from Larnaca, through Limassol to Paphos, was about 120 kilometres of twisting single track tarmac in those days. If you met anything coming the other way it was 2 wheels off and 2 wheels on to pass. The edges of the tarmac suffered from the heavy lorries and the hot sun, and in places the drop onto the loose stones and dirt on the sides was quite considerable. Having got 2 wheels off it was quite a job to find a place to get them back on. Combined with a death wish on behalf of other drivers, the occasional flock of sheep and goats ambling across, and the increasing size of lorries, it remained an exhilarating start to holidays for some years.

The warm air blowing through the window of the car brought with it first the scent of citrus groves, then mimosa, finally changing to the pungent scent of cedars as we neared Paphos. On through sleeping villages, past startled donkeys blinking in the headlights, and down onto a rough cinder track running so close to the sea the spray from crashing breakers drifted across the road.

Up another hill and then "Here is Coral Bay", and the taxi pulled up with a flourish of stones. Silence descended. The moon vanished, pitch dark surrounded us. "Where you go now?" Where indeed. "Eh, Villa

Gilks?" "Is all?" "Is all". "You follow", and we hastily eased ourselves out from under the luggage and started after him towards a barely discernible building on the skyline. As we got nearer we could see, silhouetted against a faint glow of dawn, a beach umbrella on the flat roof shading a bed. "Eh - Panicos, Villa Gilks?" bellowed our taxi driver. A gabble of Greek from the bed. "You follow", and we were off again back the way we had come, through some bushes and there was Villa Gilks, perched right on the edge of the cliff overlooking the bay.

A wonderful two weeks followed exploring the Greek half of the island, all confirming my feeling that this was where I could spend the rest of my life. There were just a few obstacles to overcome. David had always said he would never like to be tied down to a holiday cottage, he and the boys liked an activity holiday, we had no spare money and there was already bad press about people acquiring property abroad and finding they had been cheated. By by the time I was hustled back up the aircraft steps the die, as far as I was concerned, was cast, and cast if possible in the Coral Bay area.

This south western part of the island is within reach of the Troodos mountains and the hill resorts where you can ski in the winter and escape the heat of the plains in the summer, and Coral Bay is only 8 miles from bustling Paphos with its markets and shops. The sandy beach and bathing is the best in the area and just along the coast is the Akamas peninsula, a wild unspoilt stretch of mountains and pine shaded valleys, hidden springs, and wild flowers of all sorts - cyclamen, irises, tulips, grape hyacinths, anemones and orchids. In the summer the hillsides are clothed in cistus and broom and low-growing indigenous bushes, and the peninsula is surrounded by a turquoise sea, the only sound bird song and the occasional jingle of goat bells on the breeze.

Coral Bay itself, a horseshoe of cliffs round a beach of coral pink sand, was already earmarked for development, with plots marked by rusting numbered boards half hidden in the undergrowth, although in 1976 only a few villas had been built, mostly owned by expats. The villas varied from small and luxurious to large and luxurious, with highly polished black marble floors, gold fittings in the bathrooms and furniture from Maples or Harrods. Lovely to look at but luckily not quite what I had in mind.

Living about the furthest possible from the sea in England, a holiday right by it seemed most attractive, but two weeks showed up the disadvantages. It was quite noisy during the day with crowds of holiday makers enjoying themselves, and at night with the wind rattling the aluminium shutters. The gentle sound of lapping waves far from lulling one to sleep became quite irritating.

At the back of Coral Bay the land sloped gently up to a range of jagged hills, and nestling in the fold was the Venetian village of Peyia. Traditional stone houses climbed up the sides of the hills, and an imposing church perched above the square with its coffee shops and tavernas. At midday in the strong sunlight the stone houses fade into the hillside, and this is what saved the village from marauding pirates we were told.

A traditional stone house consists of one long living and sleeping room, perhaps with room at the end for animals, or with separate sheds. The flat roofs used to have a layer of mud on top of reeds laid onto rafters, cool in summer and warm in winter, although many of them had already been replaced by concrete. We did see a few in isolated places which still had the soil roof, with grass and wild flowers growing on top, and even a goat enjoying a tasty meal, perhaps put up there to act as a lawn mower. I felt this might be taking my dream a bit far, but certainly villas and black marble floors were not for us.

Back in England a cold wet summer and an even colder wetter winter helped my cause, and infiltrating my idea of a place in the sun was much easier than I had thought, although I have noticed David has since gone a bit pale if I start a sentence with "I've been thinking." The following Easter we were back out armed with the name and address, courtesy of David's barber, of a dentist in Paphos who had just what we were looking for, very cheap, very nice, very traditional, all of which turned out to be true except it was a pile of rubble in the middle of a cluster of modern apartments miles from the sea. We had also seen an advertisement in the Observer for a company called Theomaria, who were selling plots or village houses for restoration.

Theo and his wife Maria were charming people, and took us on long treks into the countryside to show us houses they had restored, beautiful but fairly unrecognizable as village houses any more because of their belief British people liked verandas and arches. Theo did show us one untouched stone house perched on a hillside but this one was also surrounded by buildings and with no view of the distant sea. Again the familiar words "No problem - I build you nice lookout". A year or so later we passed through the village and although we could not see the house, we knew where it must be as poking out of the houses was a narrow tower, like a chimney, with a ladder up one side and a small viewing platform at the top.

Our standing had gone up amongst the residents of Coral Bay when they heard David was a doctor, and we came under pressure to consider a plot there. It went up even more when I said one plot would not be big enough, we would need two at least, but fell out of sight when I said we needed the space for a village oven and sheds for a few sheep and a donkey . . . . I was assured the Residents Committee would not allow it.

Finally, with time running out, we followed up our last lead, an advertisement in the Cyprus Airways inflight magazine, for a travel company called Boadicea who also sold plots and houses for renovation. We were shown into an office where a large Scotsman behind a large desk fixed us with a beady eye whilst I rambled on about looking for an old stone house, we did not mind the condition, we just wanted to make it beautiful again. He cut me short. "Tell me what you actually want, where you want it, and how much money have you got for it."

We all chipped in our personal needs - "It has to be old, in the Peyia area above Coral Bay, not in a village but with a view of the sea, and the mountains, and a balcony, and a yard with a village oven, and a fig tree, - and not more than a couple of thousand pounds". No prizes for guessing who put in that last bit. A lengthy silence ensued from the other side of the desk. Suddenly he bounced out of his seat. "I've just the one which might suit." We were piled into a pick-up and without another word he hurtled out of Paphos, along the coast, turned up the road behind Coral Bay nearly to Peyia village and turned sharp left down a stony track back towards the sea.

As we came round a corner there I saw it, an old stone house, silhouetted against the distant blue of the sea, two stories high in the centre, with wooden steps up to a balcony.   There were stone sheds either side of a courtyard which had trees of some sort, and poking through the undergrowth was the top of a village oven. Under the edge of the top storey flat roof ran a line of square holes occupied by cooing pigeons.

"That's it" I shouted.   "That's just what we want."   "You shouldn't say that" growled Mr. Boadicea, "I could gazump you."   We clambered over the fallen archway into the courtyard.   The doors on the sheds hung on by a thread and the yard vanished into a jungle of weeds towards a small ravine.   The boys had already started to explore.   "You can see the sea." "You can see the mountains."   "There's a fig tree." "There's an ALMOND tree."

On the right of the courtyard were double wooden doors leading into a room 30 foot long by 10 foot wide with a concrete floor.   One end was a little shuttered window, and at the other a raised stone plinth had a fireplace set into the wall.   The ceiling was rough hewn wooden planks supported by old rafters, dark with age, and in the dusty gloom I could see a hugh clay amphora, the sort used for centuries to store wine.

"Kitchen area, living room, dining area."   Mr. Boadicea waved his hand up and down.   Out into the courtyard, up the wooden stairs creaking under our weight, and onto the balcony, avoiding the gaps in the planking, and through yet more double doors into a room which took my breath away.   A high wooden ceiling, soft cream flagstones, "Cyprus marble" came a growl from behind me, and a little recessed cupboard in one wall with a door hanging off. Throwing open the shutters there was a view of fields and carob trees, stretching down to the sea a mile and a half away. A soft breeze wafted the scent of herbs past me as I hung out of the window opening. Shouts of excitement from the yard and I reluctantly shut the shutters and turned to leave the room. A pigeon flew past me out of the doors, and I saw it had laid an egg in the cupboard. "You'll not need the shops here." Another growl still with a straight face.

The room underneath was as large and also had double doors, but had obviously been used for animals or storage, as it still had straw on the floor. A separate shed on the side had a distinct smell of goat, and on the other side of the courtyard the last little room was similar but smelt more of donkey.

Another fast and silent ride back to the Boadicea offices, with the awful suspense of wondering how much this beautiful house was going to cost. Mr. Boadicea, who turned out to be called Charles Dickie, a Scotsman married to Loulla, a strikingly beautiful Cypriot, sat us down in front of his desk again. A man of few words as we would come to know, they were always worth listening to. "Right," he said, "I'll tell you what you have got and what you will need to do." Somehow he also seemed to realise that all sense had fled as far as I was concerned, the house was already mine! "It will cost you £4,000 as it stands. Your walls are good, but Cyprus sandstone is soft, you will need them pointed outside, and unless you wish to live with all the creepy crawlies of the island you'll need the walls plastered inside. Your roofs are sound concrete but all flat roofs tend to crack and leak, you'll need to keep an eye on them. You have no electricity, so that will save you a penny or two, but you have mains water in the yard. I would not rely on your cooking facilities too much." So much for the village oven.

"We'll talk it over." "We'll have it." "YES" from the 3 boys. There followed three days of suspense. Two days left of our holiday and at last when we called into the offices there were the various deeds, land registration papers, and our plot marked out on a map drawn up by Lord Kitchener and still used, all to be signed by every interested or affected party which seemed to be numerous but essential. I had already been to the Bank of England before we left London to arrange the dollar premium payable in those days, and to have £2,000 cash available at the Bank of Cyprus in Paphos just in case. Visiting the Bank of England was quite an experience in itself, but the Old Lady of Threadneedle Street lived up to her reputation. The man I saw was very concerned that I was 'sailing into uncharted waters', and was I really sure I knew what I was doing. Later I sent him a picture postcard of one of the village houses all falling down with a goat on the flowery roof, which probably confirmed his direst predictions.

With one full day left the House of Solomon as it was called, was ours. We took a picnic lunch with us and off we went. I do have to say at this point that although the second sight of the house was just as wonderful, a more careful and thorough look round it was rather more intimidating, but David and the boys set to work with great enthusiasm if with little result, pulling up weeds, brushing off pigeon droppings, and shovelling years of manure out of the various sheds with a broken spade. With the double doors open in the living room I found a long wooden plank with 12 saucer shaped indentations which turned out to be where the dough was put before the bread went into the oven. In the gloom at the far end I found an old settle, the wood still in good condition, stuffed traditionally with dried weed and pebbles from the shore. We perched precariously on the verandah steps to eat our lunch, when with a sound of giggling a small boy, pushed in the back by a slightly larger girl, appeared round the corner of the house, their hands full of fruit which they unloaded into my lap. Then from the other side a little figure in black appeared, with a piece of haloumi, the local cheese, rolled up in her apron. These were our neighbours, due to become part of our lives for the next 23 years or so, and to give us so much more than a continual supply of seasonal food. They welcomed us into their families and their lives, and taught us a way of life that stretched back to a time when people thought nothing of sharing their last crust, and showed us how much we have lost in our so-called progress.

But all this was in the future. Somehow we had to find a further £2,000, and then more money for the urgent work on the house, which as far as I was concerned meant an indoor flushing lavatory to replace the hole in the ground in the yard, even though it had a marvellous view down the valley. We ventured up to the village taverna in the evening, rather fearful that the locals might resent us buying such a lovely old house. After all, at home some of the Welsh had started burning the second homes bought by the English. The taverna consisted of rickety tables with a fearsome hole in the wall at the side belching smoke and flames. After we sat down I noticed I was the only woman, a state of affairs which was quite usual then. Women did not go out in the evening, certainly not to the coffee shops or tavernas, which were definitely male territory. The women stayed home and seemed pleased to do so, especiallly when television reached Peyia.

There are never any menus in proper village tavernas, you just indicate you wish to eat, and at some time during the evening there is a sudden flurry of activity, red hot pieces of charcoal are fished out of the hole in the wall and plonked onto a grill, and haloumi, sheftalia (minced lamb in a caul) and chops, both pork and lamb, are placed on top. A vast bowl of assorted salad in season arrives on the table, drenched in olive oil with feta cheese on top, a big tub of plain yoghourt and a round of local bread to keep you going till the food is cooked. To finish there is usually a plate of fruit in season, sometimes plucked from the top of a loaded cart as it creeps down the hill past the taverna. The Keo beer in Cyprus has won medals all over the world and is a really nice light beer. The wine, red and white, can also be good, but they find it difficult to achieve quality control; a pity, as there is such a surplus of grapes.

While we were sitting wondering how to go about informing the local community we had bought a house down the hill, and was it all right, a bottle of wine arrived on the table. Trying to tell the owner of the taverna we had not ordered it, we discovered he spoke quite good English, having been a cook at the British base in Akrotiri for some years. He told us the wine was from some men sitting in the corner to welcome us to the village and wish us many happy years in the House of Solomon. Plucking up courage to ask if anyone minded us buying it there was general laughter. "No young people want old houses, they want new with marble floors and bathrooms!" Gradually everyone moved tables and pulled up chairs round us, and we were subjected to an indepth interrogation. How old were we, what work did David do, how much did he earn, and most importantly, how much did we pay for the house. We then discovered the house seemed to have belonged to most of the people there, either through an Aunt or Uncle once or twice removed, or a grandfather or some other close relative. It took us some years to find out that they were all speaking the truth, as most of the village is related in some way to each other, the taverna owner for instance is the brother of our neighbour on one side, and Katerina, the little lady in black with a flock of sheep on the other side, was married to their father's brother, and that was just for a start. More bottles of wine appeared and then bottles of brandy, which people seemed to drink like wine. With many handshakes and cries of Kalinichta (goodnight) and Sto kalo, (till we see you again), we fell into the car and somehow made it down the hill to Coral Bay.

Next day as the plane rose up into the sky over the dusty red Pendactylos mountains and crossed the tip of the Akamas Peninsula outlined in a frill of white lace edging the turquoise sea, I knew it would be over a year before we would be back again. It was a wrench to leave that time, and after 50 such leave takings it is still a wrench. When I look back I am amazed we ever managed to buy the house, and even more that over the years we were able to do so much to it by remote control.

It involved an awful lot of trust on both sides, Charles Dickie waiting patiently for the drips and drops of money we sent out when we could, and on our side by ordering various work to be done as and when we could afford it, only seeing the end result on our yearly summer holidays. We did receive an occasional photo, but sometimes it caused more concern than joy. What were the strange objects being held over a bonfire in the yard for instance? They turned out to be pigeon squabs taken from the holes under the roof before the holes were blocked up, roast squab being a local delicacy. Unfortunately, even with their living quarters blocked, generations of pigeons insist to this day in trying to find any orifice round the house to set up home, causing havoc to David's yearly fight to keep the paintwork in good condition, pigeon droppings being notoriously acid. Over the years the house has at times acquired the look of a place under siege, with rolls of wire netting shoved into any vacant places, and various other defences recommended as the ultimate deterrent. This included at one time a large inflatable owl.

The rolls of netting were immediately turned into tenements by sparrows and the local huntsmen used the owl for target practice, but only after it had been used as a perch by the pigeons and had become covered in a thick layer of guano.

At last, August the following year and we set off for Cyprus again, this time to our own house. During the previous 18 months we had got the living room walls concreted, an archway knocked through into the cowshed which had been divided in half, one half boasting, we were told, a traditional shallow sink, and the other half a bath, handbasin and lavatory. Luckily under a 2 foot depth of manure there was a concrete floor, and the walls had also been concreted. We had also apparently purchased 3 single beds put temporarily in the living room, and a double bed for the upstairs room which luckily already had plastered walls. Having been told we would only need sheets I took them with us wondering whether we would be warm enough, but I was unable to get blankets into the cases as they were full of paint brushes, tins of emulsion, a kettle, cutlery and a frying pan. In fact if we had though Easter was warm, August was like a furnace, and the boys eventually proved you could fry an egg on the beach by doing just that on a rock at mid-day.

We all adapted to the lack of electricity, using the candles provided until we got some hurricane lamps, great hissing monsters. Luckily David had been in charge of such lamps at his school during the war. To our surprise we had hot water, as solar heating panels had been installed, heavily subsidised by a far-seeing government. Unfortunately we discovered as the years went on that we did not have constant water. The division of the island during the troubles between Turks and Greek Cypriots in 1974 left the most fertile agricultural land on the Turkish side, together with a large amount of hotels and seaside resorts. On the Greek side increasing efforts were made to irrigate what had previously been land only suitable for carobs and a few olives, particularly in our part of the island, and plantations of citrus fruit, bananas, potatoes and onions sprang up. More and more hotels and houses were built to replace those lost in Kyrenia and Famagusta, and the demands on the available water grew and grew. Dams were built but failed to fill adequately, and the main source of water, the yearly snow fall high in the Troodos, became less each year. Lessons learnt in Cyprus to conserve water were applied with glee in England by David when we were put on a water meter, but somehow "If it's yellow let it mellow, if it's brown flush it down" does not have the same ring in this country.

We managed to obtain a small and erratic gas fridge and a gas stove. The gas cylinders are also subsidised by the government and after the initial purchase of a cylinder to have it replaced is extremely cheap, although it can be quite a traumatic experience to be in the middle of cooking a meal late at night and the gas runs out. The village oven which I was so keen to have in the yard turned out to be a mixed blessing. Built from the local stone it is a great dome shaped oven on a waist high plinth, with a stone or metal slab to prop over the wide opening at the front. A terracotta pot with a narrow neck and the bottom knocked out is placed in the top of the dome to form a chimney. On bread baking day, usually once a week, a large fire is lit inside the oven some hours before it is needed. When the oven has reach the desired temperature the glowing ashes are swept to one side with a bunch of olive twigs and the loaves of bread which have been proving in the long boards are placed inside with a wooden paddle. The slab of stone or tin is placed in front. If the bread bakes too quickly you can control the temperature with a flick of the olive twigs dipped in water. After the bread is taken out, again using the paddle, dough mixed with lumps of haloumi or olives are put in, or sometimes pans of meat and potatoes left in to cook slowly. More often a smaller oven called a kleftiko, made from a big terracotta pot covered with a mixture of mud and lime or concrete, is used for the meat and potatoes. The same technique is used, firing up the inside of the pot to the right temperature, putting in a parcel of lamb, potatoes and herbs, sealing up the entrance and leaving it to cook until the meat drops off the bone. For village weddings this was a favourite dish and to cope with large numbers of guests, counted in their hundreds, mobile kleftiko ovens are used, the pots being set in concrete in old wheel barrows. I was told the word kleftiko comes from the Greek word meaning thief (hence kleptomania). Some bad men stole a sheep and lit a fire to roast it. They heard people coming to look for it, scraped mud and earth over the fire and sheep, and left it. When they were able to come back hours later and uncover it they found it had cooked to perfection! The draw-back to my village oven was the amount of wood needed to get it hot enough, and the amount of bread you need to bake to fill it. It is all or nothing, and my efforts with a few twigs in the middle of its great echoing cavern reduced my next door neighbour Katerina to ill-concealed mirth. A few days later I woke up before dawn to hear what I thought at first was a fresh invasion by the Turks. Looking over the edge of the verandah I could just make out a large piece of tree moving slowly down the yard. With a great heave it was tossed to the ground and there was the little black-clad figure of Katerina. She scurried back out of the yard and I got back into bed. Not for long. Another 3 large lumps of tree later I gave up and went down into the yard to see what she was up to. Leaping about with excitement she dragged me over to the oven and pushed my head inside. "Fou fou, fou fou," she kept shouting. All I could see in the dim light of dawn was a pile of leaves and twigs. Hauling me back out she inserted her own head and shoulders and started blowing gently at the pile of leaves - a thin wisp of smoke rose up and then a flame. For the next hour ever bigger bits of tree were thrown into the gaping oven maw. Smoke now poured out of the top through the terracotta pot and the inside of the oven was beginning to glow red hot. Propping up the slab of stone over the entrance she dashed off up the track to her house and jogged back with the long bread plank on her head, the loaves already beautifully risen in the 12 round indentations. Grabbing a bunch of twigs from the olive tree overhanging the yard she tied them onto a thick stick, and then swept a large area of the oven floor clear of ash. Dipping a few more twigs into a bucket of water she flicked some drops onto the floor where they bounced and hissed, this seemed to be the equivalent of spitting on the irons in my grandmother's day. In went the bread and up went the slab in front. I took the opportunity of the natural break to get dressed while she nipped back to her house to feed the cats, hens, turkeys, rabbits, dog, pig and donkey, and to see her husband off with their flock of sheep.

Half an hour later she was back shouting for me to "Ella, ella" (come, come). The slab was removed, the paddle thrust in and out came the loaves beautifully brown, perfectly cooked, and smelling superb. The smell roused the men in my family who staggered out into the yard like the bisto kids. Leaving me two loaves she loaded up her plank with the remaining 10 and made off up the track with her paddle under her arm. The sun was well up and beginning to feel as hot as the cooling oven. As we sat under the shade of the almond tree and I watched the two loaves vanish like snow in June I thought of the work that had gone into them. Katerina had grown her wheat, harvested it, taken it to the miller on her donkey, collected bits of wood, made up her dough, and fired up the oven. For making and cooking the bread she had been up since 3 o'clock, and it was now 8.30. The village oven was already beginning to be a thing of the past when we bought our house, but over the last few years tourism has saved them from being left to crumble. Katerina has long since given up using our oven, so each year we have to clear the weeds off the top, keep the fig tree cut back so the roots don't undermine the plinth, and burn some rubbish in it to deter the insect life.

During the next few years and on our two weeks annual holiday the house gradually took shape. The goat and donkey sheds were made sound and the earth floors were covered in marble crazy paving, courtesy of the piles of broken pieces dumped in Coral Bay outside the smart villas being built there. All the wood work was painted thalassa (sea) blue, and if we ran out we just showed our legs and hands to the man in the paint shop in Paphos and he matched the colour. He also ran a framing business and took a personal interest in our house, insisting on presenting us with pictures for the walls, most of which I have to say were pretty fearful, prints of Burford, a dreadful dark crucifixion, and a badly drawn picture of some local weed. We had them hanging on the walls for many years as he was always saying he would call one day, until one year we went down to the paint shop to find he had died some months previously. The pigeons who lived on the towers of paintpots had been evicted along with the paint, and a smart shop full of plastic toys was there instead. Much as we missed him I thought at last we could get rid of the pictures, but when we tried to take them down the little pink gekos who lived behind them had nowhere to go so we have had to leave them up.

It took me a little bit of time to learn to live with the local livestock but after 23 years I think we have come to a certain level of understanding. Allowances have to be made for the fact we are only living in the house a couple of times a year, and unless family and friends use it, it then stands empty with eager squatters just waiting to move in. The pigeons who wish to nest have gradually got the message except for a pair who, when we finally got electricity, insisted on building on the electricity meter box just outside the kitchen door. The mess from a couple of chicks and the parent birds is indescribable, and as it is where we leave the keys, messages, fuses etc., every time we lift the lid an avalanche of droppings, feathers and twigs falls off, while the chicks cling on for dear life and the parent birds have hysterics. We have tried putting sharp objects on top, loose large stones, netting it all in, prickly thorn branches, jelly as used in London, moving the nest to a suitable place. Nothing works. Our last visit we got a local carpenter to build a ski-slope wooden top to the box, so we shall see . . . As for the rest of the local pigeons, they arrive at dawn on the flat roof above our bed and practice a sophisticated marching routine in hobnail boots, ending with loud squawks as they void their bowels over the edge of the roof onto David's freshly painted bannisters. If there was any lingering doubt in the minds of our neighbours that the British are mad the sight of David bursting out of the bedroom in his pyjamas screaming and shouting and shaking his fist at the sky confirms all their suspicions.

While on the subject of droppings the bats also have no need of a high-fibre diet. When we discovered we had a pair of flittermice living in the gap of the verandah roof over the entrance to our bedroom we were delighted. As dusk fell they would fly in and out over our heads as we sat watching the sun go down, helping to keep down the mosquitoes. But over the years a pair has become a dozen, three dozen, six dozen, until there must have been over a hundred.   They streamed out over our heads squeaking and squawking and yes, you have guessed it, voiding their bowels after a long day sleeping.   At least it dropped as fine rain in the case of the bats, but it really got a bit much.   Again we tried to persuade them gently to move on and out. At great expense we had a bat box made.   David nailed it up round the side of the house but the only things we got in it were sparrows.   We had another design from the bat preservation society made up at yet more expense with a similar result.   When I rang them to report back they said yes, it was strange, they had sold plenty of bat boxes but were still waiting to hear of any being occupied.   Luckily overcrowding eventually forced the bats to fresh pastures and we hastily filled in the hole.   The fruit bats are no problem.   They come and feed in the fig tree when the figs are ripe, and except for the splat as a ripe fig hits the yard seem to have the decency to save any bodily functions till they return to their roost which is luckily not on our property. However there is a hazard to be avoided.   Returning late at night on our motorbike David has been hit in the face once or twice by a disorientated fruit bat, which he likens to being swiped with a leather handbag.   These bats are big.

The house lizards look after themselves although they are inclined to be noisy at night and conduct lengthy conversations from behind one picture to another.   As long as one allows their discreet droppings to dry before trying to brush them off the white walls one can avoid a nasty brown smear and a fresh outburst from the house decorator.

The ants, again within reason as to quantity, can be very useful indeed.   They range from extremely large to minute and can be harnessed to act as an efficient hoover, preferably outside. It is always wise to lift bare feet off the ground after a meal and then one can enjoy the sight of a large crumb moving by itself across the yard. It never ceases to amaze me how such tiny creatures can move such large objects, and within half an hour the ground under the table is clean. As long as one is scrupulous indoors in keeping work tops and table tops absolutely clear of anything sweet and sticky all is well, and having swatted the odd insect or two it is nice to see the body being carried out of the kitchen door.

The hornets are large, and I treat them with respect. They like to drink from the tap in the yard twice a day and I give them a clear berth. The only other time they are a nuisance is when the grapes growing on the arbour are ripe, and I try and avoid this by picking off the flowers or newly formed bunches in the Spring. It seemed a bit drastic at first, but we only need the vines for shade, and we get given a lot of much better quality grapes.

When it came to the garden itself I learnt by trial and error what could go without water from Spring to Autumn. It was no good casting envious eyes on the lush gardens of the Coral Bay villas with their exotic flowering shrubs. We already had an almond and a fig tree, and right at the start I had asked for a lemon and a kitromila (or marmalade orange) tree to be planted. The builders put in a lemon and a sweet orange tree, marmalade not being considered a priority. Never mind, they looked lovely and I looked forward to picking my very own lemons and oranges. Unfortunately, just as they were beginning to fruit, a neighbour decided the trees were no good, and grafted a mandarin and grapefruit on instead. Very kind, but it meant another few years wait. Then someone from the village passing by noticed they were not what I had wanted, and grafted on lemons and oranges again. Another few years and Katerina, obviously having looked forward to mandarins, cut it all off again and grafted both trees with mandarins. I took the hint and went and bought myself a lemon and orange tree and hid them at the end of the yard. At last I have managed to pick enough oranges and lemons to make 5 small pots of marmalade. Who cares whether it is mandarin or grapefruit, orange or lemon, the perfume from the blossom and the brilliant colours of the fruits against the rich green leaves are a constant delight.

And as for flowers, I have given up the fight against nature, geraniums are the answer. Not the weedy little specimens in England, costing an arm and a leg from the nurseries each year, but great clumps of sprawling red, magenta and pink, needing to be attacked with shears each Autumn.

The boys have had a wonderful time each year, slowly filling in the yard with flat stones and concrete, and building a table and barbeque under the trees. Various other projects were started, some successful and some not, including a small windmill to generate electricity, but all giving them many hours of constructive pleasure. Gradually this gave way to increasing interest in girls, and the final test of a future wife seemed to be to bring her out to the House of Solomon. Each one of my 3 delightful daughters-in-law passed this test, and also Katerina's, which seemed to involve assessing future child bearing potential from the gestures. Perhaps it came from being a shepherdess. When you think I have never been able to understand a word Katerina has said to me nor she a word I have said to her it is amazing how easily we have managed to communicate. At one point she told our plumber she could not understand why I could not speak Greek, even the babies in Cyprus could.

She has taught me how to make haloumi, tiri and anari, all various cheeses from her ewes' milk; trahanas which is a mixture of sour milk and ground wheat, shaped with a specially cut piece of bamboo from the ravine and dried in the sun for use in soups in the winter; soushouko, a grape sweet, and many more traditional dishes. I have helped her harvest carobs, shell almonds and crack olives. How to milk a reluctant sheep might not be so useful. You hang on to a back leg and whack it with a plastic bucket till it stands still!

It was a lovely sight to see the flock go out every day. The milking sheep had multicoloured pieces of cloth like one cup bras tied over their udders, while the new lambs were left in a shed to sleep quietly through the heat of the day. Hunger would wake them eventually and the chorus of baas would gradually gather volume. Katerina would hear the flock coming in the distance and let the lambs out. Down the hill would come the flock with the mothers leading the field, and the lambs would scamper to meet them. Katerina's husband wore the traditional white shirt, baggy black trousers and knee length black boots. He carried his stick across his shoulders with his arms draped over it, and controlled his flock of 40 or so sheep just by calling softly to them.

He must have been in his eighties when he died. His eyesight had been failing, and the ram, always an uncertain quantity, had gored his leg. Katerina had moved him into a shelter in her yard to catch the sea breezes and we were summoned to pay a formal visit to his bedside. A hen was perched on the bedrail and various cats were keeping him company. After he died Katerina struggled on with an ever-decreasing number of sheep. Finally her family removed the last few, more as a kindness to the sheep, and possibly to us, than Katerina. They lived in a corrugated shed, and as dawn was breaking she used to take great delight in running her stick up and down the corrugations shouting and yelling "Ella, ella." No calling to them softly, they were sent on their way with the odd well-aimed lump of rock. I would stagger hastily to the door of our bedroom to return her greeting as she passed before she rattled her stick along our freshly painted gate and David leapt out of bed to carry out his muttered threats.

I had to remind him Katerina had her uses. Although our yard looked lovely when freshly swept, and a nice green hedge had been encouraged to grow on the edge of the ravine marking our boundary with Katerina on the other side, the winter rains caused havoc. Mud was washed down the track through our yard and into the ravine. By the time we came out in the Spring the sun had already baked the residue rock hard and weeds were already taking hold. If I did a bit of shovelling each day, and covered the blisters up as they appeared, I could get it all cleared and swept just before we returned to England. When the track was concreted a deluge then roared down the half mile of concrete, turned sharp left and right through our gate, and washed bits of the hedge into the ravine each year till even the corner of the house was threatened with subsidence. We needed a wall, starting at the bottom of the ravine, and finishing about 4 feet above the level of what was left of the flower bed.   Far too big and expensive to be built of the local stone it also needed to be extra strong.   It would have to be concrete and reinforcing rods.

Now Cypriots have an affinity with concrete close to an obsession.   They love it.   In time the whole island will be covered in it.   They have an everlasting supply under the ground of the raw materials and daily vast amounts are dug up, bagged up, and sent round the island on hugh lorries.   Concrete-mixers range from women in flowered overalls and sun hats with a shovel, through battered little mixers that can be hitched to the back of a car, to enormous ship's boiler size, a vast load on the back of a straining lorry, sloshing and rolling, with the chute clanging against the side urging it on.

So the local population's eyes glowed at the mere mention of us wanting a concrete wall.   However, beating off all opposition Katerina secured the contract to build it, or that is how we translated her barrage of Greek.   It was to be no problem, could be done before we left by her son Hambi, her grandson had access to a concrete mixer and she would personally supervise.   As usual it seemed to be rude of us to mention money or timing.   Four days left of our holiday and we were resigned to re-opening negotiations the following year when we woke as dawn was breaking to what I thought was an earthquake.   With a tremendous roar and clatter a lorry was tipping up a hugh pile of shuttering into the yard.   Another lorry was waiting on the track to back down with a load of rusting reinforcing rods.   We got some clothes on but by that time the clothes line and swimming costumes, a couple of garden chairs and a yard broom had vanished under the pile of rods.   The lorries had gone and the dust was settling.   By the end of the day we were wondering whether the lorries had delivered to the wrong house. Katerina had been strangely absent, and the next day was equally quiet. Two days to go. We were having breakfast, perched with difficulty on the remaining chairs on what was now a building site, when a pick-up truck clattered to a halt outside the gate. Hambi had arrived complete with his work force, Katerina. Always smiling, and always ready to help out a friend in need, her son works all hours to earn money to send his children to university, and he is certainly an expert with shuttering and reinforcing rods. What I had not bargained for was both David and myself being part of the work force. Under Katerina's direction we hauled shuttering and rods into position all day long, having discovered that "tomorrow is coming the concrete early, is no stopping." And the concrete did come early, one of those hugh lorries with chute, which the grandson fixed to the end of the shuttering. If we thought we had worked hard the day before getting the shuttering ready it was nothing to how fast and hard we had to work to keep the concrete flowing along to the end of it. And here Katerina came into her own. Armed with a large plank she paddled the concrete along shouting at us "Grigora, grigora" (quickly,quickly). In the heat concrete sets quickly, and once these hugh lorries start to spew out their contents you can't seem to stop it. Not wishing to be shown up by someone in her late seventies we did our best, helped by Hambi and his son, but it was touch and go, and certainly if, as I remind David, Katerina had not been foreman we would have had more of a rockery than a wall.

We have seen our neighbours' children grow up and have children, and now there are even great-grandchildren. Things are quieter the other side of the ravine, and we listen anxiously each time we arrive at the House of Solomon until we hear Katerina's voice rising up as she sweeps a clutter of cats out of her door. Now in her eighties (she thinks) she broke her hip recently and was in an old people's home for a short while, but hated it as "they are all old".

It is hard to believe how the years have flown, life moves on and changes have to be faced with it. David is right, we shall have to think about selling the House of Solomon. He has been retired now for some years, years filled with the fun of being together, enjoying travelling, seeing more of family and friends. But everything is beginning to take much longer and is more of an effort. I just hope that whoever buys the house will have as much pleasure from it as we have.

Our own 3 sons and wives have produced 6 grandsons and 1 grandaughter so far for us to play with, all of course the brightest and best. I know how blessed I am, but in the back of my mind the plight of the AIDS children in Romania haunts me still.

Dr. Matusa struggles on still with over six hundred children and families in various stages of HIV and AIDS. Most of the children I knew have died, but Daniella, when I last heard, was still going strong, in spite of lungs ravaged by TB. Many of the surviving children are in their early teens now, and many are being cared for within their families. The needs have changed, and Christine, ever resourceful, is trying to meet these changes. Plans are underway for a clinic in Constanta with AIDS outpatient facilities to include a dental unit, something sadly lacking for the AIDS children because of the danger. There will be a terminal unit with family facilities and a chapel of rest.

Christine has found a building and it is being renovated. She is busy raising funds to equip and run it, hopefully under the experienced management of Sheila Donaghy who ran the hospice so well in the early days. It will be under the direction of Dr. Matusa, and my other dear friend Dr. Liliana Popescu, now Deputy Minister of Health for the Constanta area, will also be involved. The Metropolitan police, including Sir John and Lady Stevens, have thrown their considerable weight into the project, together with the usual financial generosity of Rotary International.

I know how much money will be needed, and I find it very frustrating that age has definitely taken its toll and I cannot get actively involved any more. As one friend so charmingly put it "Let's face it, you are no longer a spring chicken, more of an old broiler"! That is why I have decided to publish this book myself and not through a publishing company, which is very hard to do these days anyway unless one is a celebrity, has slept with a president or embezzled a few million. This way every penny I get for the book will go towards equipment or medicine to help these dying children. Perhaps a final poem I wrote one Christmas will explain how I feel.

Christmas over and I am putting Squeezy in my turkey pan.
Woosh it goes across the surface,
Pushing bits and grease away into the corners and down the sink.
How I wish I could sprinkle Squeezy on my mind.

Ten years ago this pan was new, untried, non-

stick unscratched,
A bit like me before Romania.
But now my mind is filled with bits and pieces
that stick like grease,
Little ghosts at all my feasts and celebrations.

Especially at Christmas. Like the film on the
surface of the water
The dead children crowd in.
When I kneel at the altar to drink from the cup
of blood on Christmas Eve
They are with me, names hard to remember, but
faces never, never.

Twisted limbs, swollen bellies, huge eyes, rat-
chewed ears
And bitten toes,
Death in their love bites, lurking in their kisses,
found in their tears,
Love sucked out of one's soul like water in the
desert sun,
Never enough.

There, Squeezy has cleaned the pan like new,
away it goes into the cupboard till next time.
Are those little ghosts to be wiped away as well?
No, welcome to my feasts and celebrations,
enrich them with your presence.
No Squeezy for you, my little loves.

It seems a long time ago when our eldest son, at
the age of 10, was asked by one of David's patients
whether he was going to be a doctor like his father, and
replied "I might, but it's no life for the wife"!